The Café after the P

The Café after the Pub after the Funeral

Hattie Gordon

continuum
LONDON • NEW YORK

Continuum
The Tower Building
11 York Road
London SE1 7NX

15 East 26th Street
New York
NY 10010

www.continuumbooks.com

First published 2003

British Library Cataloguing-in-Publication Data
A catalogue record for this book is available from the British Library

ISBN 08264–7016–5 (hardback)

Typeset by Fakenham Photosetting Ltd, Fakenham, Norfolk NR21 8NN
Printed and bound in Great Britain by MPG Books Ltd, Bodmin, Cornwall

For Dad and Callum

Acknowledgements

Thanks go to staff at the Royal Free Hospital, the Northgate Clinic, and the Tavistock Clinic; to Robin Baird-Smith; to Mark Bostridge; to unofficial editors, you know who you are, in particular, Alice Hartmann, Emily Kyriakides and Tamsin Leigh; to protectors, partners in crime and soulmates, always shining diamonds; to Anthony, for years of loving arms. *Ti voglio bene*; to my father, and to Callum for his unflinching loving support.

The lines from Poem VII of *Twenty-One Love Poems.* Copyright © 2002 by Adrienne Rich. Copyright © 1978 by W. W. Norton & Company, Inc, from The Fact of a Doorframe: Selected Poems 1950–2001 by Adrienne Rich. Used by permission of the author and W. W. Norton & Company, Inc.

ICD–10 Classification of Mental Behavioural Disorders: Somatization Disorder and Borderline Type is used by permission of WHO.

References

For historical information on suicide I have chiefly relied upon A. Alvarez's *The Savage God: A Study of Suicide,* Penguin: 1971, and Kay Redfield Jamison's *Night Fall's Fast: Understanding Suicide,* Picador: 2000.

What kind of beast would turn its life into words?
What atonement is this all about?
– and yet, writing words like these, I'm also living.

Adrienne Rich, Poem Seven, from *Twenty-One Love Poems 1974–1976*

His body dreams
towards night.

The nightmare breaks
when outside the pub
laughter
spills into fear.

The sound will ever remain.

Giles Gordon, Poem Six, from *Eight Poems for Gareth,* 1970

Gareth, Hattie and Callum photographed by Fay Godwin in the doorway of the family home

Chapter One

It was six years after my mother's death. My father and his new young family had moved south of the river. I was in his house running a bath when the pitch of the doorbell filled its rooms and hallways. Having seen through the window two policemen walk towards the house, Dad's childminder shouted up the stairs to me, 'I think it's the police.' I knew what they were about to tell me before I opened the door. I did not need to see their faces, let alone hear their words, because I already knew. It had been a long time coming. The repetition was ruthless, the men of law and order who spread knowledge of death, here once again. The pattern was macabre. There were two of them, only this time they were fully aware. I opened the door, and the figures before me in that blue so dark it is almost black asked if they could come in. I didn't want them to be the ones to tell me, so I asked, 'Is it about Gareth?'

'Yes, I'm afraid it is, madam.'

'Is he dead?'

'I'm afraid he is, madam.'

My brother had killed himself. He was discovered on Tuesday, 13 September 1994 in his flat by Primrose Hill. When they found his body the police noted a newspaper in his living room that was dated for the previous Thursday. They forced open his front door after his neighbours downstairs reported a foul stench emanating from the floor above them. I pictured the police with a crowbar, wrenching open the sealed door, closed from the inside by his own hand. Cracking the wood so that paint flaked off and splintered. He would have had no idea how long his body would be there before it was found. He'd made sure no one else had keys to his flat.

I said something daft to the policemen, about how it must be hard for them to tell people that someone has died. They weren't interested in responding to me, they wanted to get out of the house. One of the officers told me I would have to telephone the station to find out the details of the case. The case. The case of my brother.

Because of the drugs he had taken his body had doubled in size. His bed was beneath a curtainless window, so the sun had hastened his decomposition. His lifeless body, changing its form by the minute as he decomposed, had evidently basked in the sun for a few days. The horror of dead flesh disintegrates with the realization that the soul that once occupied it has fled.

We don't know the exact date of his death.

His poor body had been attacked on and off for the latter half of his twenty-four years. Overdoses of anti-depressants, painkillers and alcohol, averaging one a year for ten years, destroyed his once intact liver. Hare-brained schemes of draining his blood with a pump led to self-inflicted incisions, and a bathroom on a psychiatric ward being sprayed with blood type O. Attempts to fall from London's highest buildings lacked valour, and instead he was found sickly drunk by police. His body was resilient, up to a point.

After overdoses, in states of drug-induced delirium, hideous monsters in an alliance of cruelty would connive to chase and catch him so that he would run from hospital beds. The tubes inserted to rouse him from his toxic state – in his eyes snakes – would be torn from his body as he attempted to outrun these demons. Panic in eyes already full and dark with dilated pupils ran riot. Unsure of whether the demons were within or without, he attacked himself to win the war. A single body became a battleground.

In Europe, until the early twentieth century, an attempt at self-murder was punishable by hanging. Around 1860 a man was hanged for failing to die when he cut his own throat.

A man was hanged who had cut his throat, but who had been brought back to life. They hanged him for suicide. The doctor had warned them that it was impossible to hang him as the throat would burst open and he would breathe through the aperture. They did not listen to his advice and hanged their man. The wound in the neck immediately opened and the man came back to life again although he was hanged. It took time to convoke the aldermen to decide the question of what was to be done. At length aldermen assembled and bound up the neck below the wound until he died.

In most European countries suicide was decriminalized during the eighteenth and nineteenth centuries. It remained a crime in England and Wales until 1961, worthy of imprisonment if an attempt failed. In Ireland, suicide was a crime until 1993; the year before Gareth died.

Under Christian and State guidance, those who committed suicide were esteemed to be as contemptible as the lowest criminal and were to be dishonoured. For centuries they were buried under crossroads, the same place used for public executions, so that the besieged soul couldn't find its way back home. The greater the traffic to keep it down, the better. A stone would be placed over the deceased's face to prevent his or her ghost from rising to haunt the living. Sometimes stakes would be driven through the heart of a suicide, just like the night's vampires, as though the dead body would otherwise mimic the blood-seeking Transylvanian creatures and rise to bite once more. The last suicide to be buried in England in this way lies at the intersection of Grosvenor Place and the King's

Road, Chelsea. It was placed there in 1823. After this time, for the next fifty years, the bodies of unclaimed and destitute suicides were sent to schools of anatomy for dissection. Lost bodies to be splayed open in the pursuit of learning.

Lose them, confuse them, leave them stranded, crossed by wheels, walked over by soles and souls that will never know.

In France, the suicide's body was dragged through the streets, face down towards the ground he or she could no longer bear to walk on, then hanged on a gallows. In the seventeenth century the law stated that after the hanging the body must be thrown either into a sewer or onto the city dump to ensure complete degradation.

In Danzig, the corpse was lowered by pulleys from the window of the building he or she had committed the act in, because it was forbidden for the suicide corpse to exit through the door. The window frame was subsequently burnt for fear of further contamination.

The suicide was buried outside the walls of Plato's Athens, and the hand, a despicable tool of self-murder, cut off and buried separately, as though keeping the body whole might incur further destruction.

Ancient Roman law prohibited the suicide's possessions and property from being passed onto heirs.

Rather than use bare hands, the Finns lifted the corpse into the coffin with pokers, otherwise curses and disease would infiltrate the family.

Traditionally, orthodox Jewish custom didn't mourn for the suicide and treated the rejecter of life as nothing, even before the corpse began to rot. Everything was done to respect the living, not honour the deceased.

In Islamic belief, suicide – murder of the self – is no different to the murder of another.

History told me to feel shame. To carry Gareth's final act as a black mark.

When the police left, in my mind appeared his face the last time I saw him. We had passed each other whilst on buses which were going in opposite directions. The buses stopped for less than a minute in a traffic jam, so that coincidentally we were facing each other. I tried to catch his attention but he failed to see me and looked right past me. He was oblivious, the glass window caught reflections from the world around him, yet he never caught sight of me. A fly buzzed against my window, hitting it repeatedly, getting nowhere new. With two sheets of glass between us I had looked at him whilst he was ignorant of being watched. I looked to gain insight into his torment. Of course I didn't find it. I saw his strong face, a hybrid of many distinguished male faces, his greenish eyes, and his great height even as he was seated. Physically he bore the strength of an ox, emotionally and psychologically he bore infinite frailty.

On several occasions when he walked London's streets police on the beat would approach him and ask what he was up to, such was his gait and imposing physicality. This disharmony between his body and his mind was an element of his misunderstood self. He could unintentionally prompt fear in others, including me, but he was plagued by fear, by the harshness of a less than gentle world, a world that mastered him more than he would ever master it.

I tried to recall what I was doing when he died. Reversing the terrain of memory, fruitlessly going back in time. Was I on the plane returning from Delhi? I had gone to India for the summer. On planes I stare at the clouds hoping to catch a glimpse of my mother, or of the celestial angels who now protect her. The Aeroflot winged tin machines, whose passengers have so little faith they

5

applaud when they land in one piece, take so very long to reach their destination. I was travelling for over twenty-four hours, stopping in the drab Moscow airport for a while on the way. He may well have passed while I was on board a plane. Or was it before, when jewellers were attempting to persuade me to import their sparkling precious gems? Faceted glass cut from soda bottles, a 7-Up bottle becomes an emerald, a clear Coke bottle becomes a diamond. Or was it when man after man could see in my eyes that his uncle had the most exquisite carpet for me? The fortune-teller grabbed me from the street. 'You have one snake eye and one parrot eye, that means you are a very lucky woman.' With incense burning and Ganesh sitting beside him, he told me all was well with my family, and that I must never eat fish on Tuesdays.

And all the while he was rotting.

In the days before I was old enough to walk to school, my mother would drive me in her battered Ford. It was striking because Callum, my other brother, had airbrushed red and orange flames on the bonnet. On a day like any other as I stepped out of that car, she leaned across to me and said, 'You do know that Gareth tried to kill himself don't you?'

'Of course,' I said, but had no clue. How would I know when you told me he was in hospital because he had had an accident? The accident had remained unidentified, and no one asked awkward questions. He was merely the Problem Child. Apparently there is always one, and more often than not it is the middle child. My heart raced as I walked through the school doors amidst the screams of the playground. It was his first overdose. He was thirteen.

When Mum picked me up from school in the flaming Ford, she told me we were going to visit Gareth in hospital. The Royal Free Hospital was a convenient five-minute drive from my primary school. Words fell out of her mouth as though she didn't want to let them go; yet she knew she couldn't take me to that place without some semblance of explanation. Cloaked in the shakes was a minimal confession that reluctantly told me he had swallowed a bottle of aspirins and washed them down with apple juice. Dumbfounded that this was happening, I absorbed the information but not the implications. I didn't register that he could have died, or that he may really have wanted to die. But I could envision the little blond boy who was pent-up with sadness, anger and frustration and didn't know what else to do but resort to the extreme.

His stomach was pumped out; he was made clean, shiny and new. He spent a couple of nights in hospital, for cautious doctors to be satisfied of his physiological recovery.

Months later he did it again and nearly died. He survived only because he was remarkably physically strong, that's what the doctors said.

A few years later Gareth took another overdose; this time they decided to keep him and he was placed in the psychiatric ward. He was seventeen. Gareth was put in an adult psychiatric ward because there wasn't room for him in the adolescent ward.

The visits to him became my after-school routine. There were just over four years between Gareth and I. By then I was in secondary school and when I got home in the afternoon my mother and I would drive to the hospital to see him. We walked up the height of the dreary spiral steps, past the ambulances, past the admissions desk, past the injured, the convalescing, the dying, and up, up in the lift. On entering the ward, more often than not, a certain shrunken pensioner would accost me. She would put her arm through mine and stay attached to me with a vengeance, as though bereft of a Siamese other half. The appearance of a hunched scrawny body betrayed her, her muscles were strong from clinging tight.

Whispering streams of mumbles with no beginning and no end, she walked me around and around the corridors of the ward that formed a continuous square. When I spoke to her it fell on her ears like a foreign language. Pigeon steps carried this little lady, slowly, slowly, never seeming to stop. She walked with us as we looked for Gareth. We would find him lying on his bed or in the day room, where patients stared into thin air; stared at any visitor; talked with each other or their visitor; or were welded to the television screen. He would tell my tenacious acquaintance that she would have to let me go because we were leaving the ward. She stood elfin and alone, head drawn to the linoleum floor with no break in her oration.

We would accompany him to the hospital cafeteria, and clamber into the seats that were fixed to the floor, presumably so they could not be thrown or stolen, and sit around the plastic table. On good days we would chat. He would tell us tales of who was having sex with whom on the ward. The result of drugs, which had aphrodisia as a side effect, was that the next Messiah would copulate with the local pyromaniac. The difficulties of pulling off a complete shag when only a clinical blue curtain separated one patient from the next were emphasized, not to mention that the curtain could of course have been set alight at any moment.

My mother, desperate for her son, would rack her thoughts for small talk. In the face of depression, psychiatry and looming suicide, she would rely on me to gloss over the anguish with talk of soap operas or gossip about our friends, and was noticeably pleased when there was something to say, no matter how trivial. Instants when there was a laugh or a smile, even for passing seconds, restored to her an impression of her son's character without complications.

But most days we would proceed to eat from vending machines in order to fill the silence. We would rather hear the clunk of coins and the rustle of crisps and chocolate packets as they dropped to the bottom of the junk machine.

To confront the truth was too much for a mother. A suicidal son. Her face was distraught, but calmer for the habitual routine. Having him there was safer, away from knives or pills. Every attempt on his life wrecked her. There was no getting used to his desire to remove himself from the world, regardless of how heartfelt the desire was. Each time the ambulance drove him away from our house she sat in the green armchair by the fireplace and her hands would be shaking. She would need tea then alcohol. Mum drank tea as though it were more vital to her than oxygen. Her side of the family were known for their stoical consumption of it. Whatever she was doing, she always had a cup in her hand. She nursed tea, as if each cup were a precious gift, pressing her palms and thin fingers around the cup, joining the slender base of her hands and the tips of her fingers for the warmth. Her eyes were veneered with resolute despair.

Even before he ended up in hospital through his overdoses, Gareth was always getting into accidents. Callum had fallen and his teeth had pierced the flesh between the bottom lip and the cleft of the chin. I had fallen in the school playground and received a scar next to my right eye. That was about the extent of our childhood injuries, but Gareth was much more accident-prone. My mother would handle each incident with staid patience and get him to the nearby casualty.

One day during the school holidays I was cooking a cake in the kitchen and Mum, a children's book illustrator, was working on drawings for a book. Suddenly Gareth burst through the downstairs door screaming his head off and clutching his finger as blood spurted out of it. Knowing that doctors could stick bits of the body back to where they should be if they became detached, he was holding a tiny part of his finger in his other hand. My mother grabbed a tea towel, wrapped it around his finger and calmly told me when to take the dinner out of the oven. She then sped him off to casualty in her car. He had been oiling the chain on his bike in a petrol station when someone knocked the bike and his finger got caught in the chain and the tip of it was cleanly sliced off.

Another time, in one of the estates near where we lived, Gareth was riding his new BMX bike through the twists and turns of the yellow-brick blocks of flats. He went down some stairs and at this crucial moment forgot that the way to brake on this new bike was to pedal backwards. At the bottom of the stairs, out of control, he went hurtling over the handlebars and knocked the ends of his front teeth clean away. He had them capped and they were a slightly different colour to the rest of his teeth, until the rest of his teeth discoloured in the years to come. Several months before he died, one of the caps fell off and he didn't get it replaced. In a way, the jagged chipped tooth suited him.

It was this bike that acted as the catalyst for his first overdose; or rather, it was events around it that led to the breakdown and depression that resulted in the overdose. When he was about twelve, Gareth discovered he had a talent for jumping on BMX bikes. He was incredible when he was on that bike of his. On a sticker stuck across the crossbar was the bike's brand name: Diamondback. Riding it, he was gifted. He won every competition that he entered, he received money and trophies, but most of all, and what seemed to be most important to him, he won the respect of everyone else who watched or jumped on those bikes in Kentish Town. He became a bit of a star. We have pictures of him riding the air on a neat twist of the front wheel and handle bars. With Gareth riding it, a jerk of the back of the bike up in the air looked like dancing heels being kicked out.

Then, high on his glory, gangs of children first stole his watch, then his Walkman. Next they threatened him with knives and stole his bike, his pride. He got the bike back but the trauma of being threatened ate away at him. Then the Diamondback broke and that was when he started to disintegrate. His dignity stolen from beneath, right when he was flying on his gift, swept away before he chose to relinquish it.

If it hadn't been the bike maybe it would have been something else. Until that point he had been difficult, sometimes violent, hyperactive and loud, then he went into himself. He refused to attend school and refused to leave the house. On the few occasions that he did leave he ducked down in the car so he couldn't be seen. He spent his days sat in his bedroom or another room in the house with the curtains closed and the mindlessness of daytime television whispering to him.

Gareth had incredibly sensitive hearing – he kept the television sound down low, kept its murmurs hushed. For someone who was so noisy in their actions and gestures, it seemed odd that he was sensitive to noise. He'd always made a lot of noise, some of it intentional, some less so. But whatever he was up to, you always knew where he was because of it.

After that first overdose, when he was sent home from the hospital, things carried on just as they were before it. Him, in hiding from living. The days stretched into weeks.

My mother then found a boarding school for Gareth. She didn't know what else to do with him and was afraid of what he might do if he lived at home. She was also scared of being alone with him in the house but was unable to leave him for fear of what actions he might take against himself.

It was a school for disturbed children. Our paternal grandfather paid for the first term with the hope that the local education authority (LEA) would take on the fees for the next term as our parents couldn't afford it. The LEA was disgruntled from the start because my mother had placed Gareth there without contacting them first. They didn't seem to grasp the extent of the desperation – that their red tape might well have inadvertently resulted in his dying. There was a huge sense of relief in the house when he started going to Arlington Hall. Mum didn't know if he would be able to stay but even without the certainty of permanence he wasn't at home so she started to feel better. She spent less time drinking and less time in bed. After a while he came home at the weekends. As each of those weekends encroached a certain dread crept under her skin but at least during the week we were largely free from trouble and she could begin to breathe again.

Gareth liked the school when he first went there, though he soon grew to hate it and renamed it the Torture Chamber. It had a farm and animals and acres of land, the idea being that the children, who all had behavioural difficulties of one kind or another, would develop responsibility towards the animals. When a litter of piglets was born Gareth was given the job of looking after them. He perked up at this point in quite a big way. He became very attached and loved taking care of them. At home he spoke about them with pride and showed us photos of them as though they were his. He went so far as to say that he might one day want to live on a farm, which was a huge step for him because the thought of facing any kind of future, even acknowledging that there might be a future, held utter terror for him. When he returned to school after the half-term holiday the pigs had been sold, taken away and turned into bacon. He was devastated; the meaning they'd given him had been replaced with resentment and loss.

The journeys to and from the school became an ordeal for my mother. She did all the driving, as our father didn't hold a licence. When we lived in County Cork, Ireland, for a few months in the 1970s when Dad was between jobs and writing a novel, and where at that time one could drive without a licence, he demonstrated how dangerous he was on the road. With the three of us in the back of the car, he asked Mum why there were cars on the wrong side of the road coming towards us. The reply came before a swift turn of the steering wheel: 'They're not on the wrong side, you are.' He'd had lessons as a young man, but his recklessness in negotiating roads had led his instructor to advise him not to take the test. So my mother would pick Gareth up every Friday night and drive him back on Sunday evening. During his most depressed bouts he would tell her that he was planning to jump out of the car when they were speeding down the motorway. True to form, Gareth carried out his threat. On one journey home he did open the door and tried to leave the zooming vehicle. She pulled onto the hard shoulder, wrestled with him, and somehow managed to keep him in the car. On the journey back, she persuaded the police to give her an escort in case he gave a repeat performance. But they only agreed to go so far, turned back after a few miles and left her to complete the drive with him alone. It was nightmarish for her. She had to get him back to the school or he might do something dangerous at home, but when taking him back he might do something equally dangerous. Gareth had a way of setting things up so that there really wasn't a better option. There was no get-out clause – the get-out clause was his death. Though for my mother the better option was to get him away from the house. If he was there things could get totally out of control, that's how she seemed to feel.

After a few years articles started appearing in newspapers. The methods used at the school were considered dubious by the Department of Health, and Social Services were warned not to send any more children to it. Sometimes the children were kept in their nightclothes during the day so that they were unable, or maybe more reluctant, to abscond. They were physically restrained if they were violent. Claims were made that the most difficult children were deprived of food and made to sit in cold rooms. Gareth said they were locked in cupboards and humiliated in front of one another, which was never mentioned in the papers. Slowly the teachers left and various educational authorities took out several of the few children they had placed there. Gareth, however, was left. I don't know if my parents disbelieved the stories – more likely my mother's sanity couldn't tolerate the thought of him, leaving for it would mean he would come home and we'd be back at the beginning. So she did nothing. Before he finished his final year he took another overdose the night before his next term was due to start and didn't return. Months later the school was closed down.

It was at Arlington Hall that Gareth started having problems with his eyes. He said they were agony, that it felt as though sandpaper was being grated against them. They burnt too, scalded his vision and his head began to throb. His eyes took over; they became his reason, his explanation. This symptom never disappeared – others succeeded it but none eclipsed this torture. It must have been too excruciating for Gareth to see – to see what was going on around him translated by the hurt inside. He didn't know how he could live, he said, when he couldn't see and was in such pain. Mum took him to Moorfields Eye Hospital, repeatedly. He was convinced cancer was living behind his eyes and eating away at them. Each time the patient staff gave him the utmost attention and each time told him there was nothing wrong. There was no cancer, said the eye doctor. My mother insisted that his eyes be checked on a regular basis.

Battling for him no matter what he did or how distraught and aggressive he was, she was like a warrior woman with Gareth. His life ate into hers. Parasitic to the end. The worst part is that her untiring perseverance never seemed to help him, though it nearly, perhaps did, destroy her.

She gave Gareth a dog because she thought it would be some comfort to him. One evening, totally unexpectedly, she and Gareth came home with a floppy white boxer puppy. Gareth named her Sniffy. He had her up in his room that first night and they bonded straight away – he was crazy about her. Though he didn't look after her, my mother did all of that, she was always his dog more than anyone else's. From the moment she came home Sniffy was at his side as he skulked about. She quickly attuned to every tension, vibe and raised voice. When there was a fight in the house she would get a raised lump on her head.

When we were walking her people would come up to us and say, 'Oh, how unusual, a white boxer. You don't see many of those do you?' It was the same comment every time. Then they'd ask what this beautiful muscular dog was called and we'd have to admit her name was Sniffy. They'd swallow their laughs as we struggled with her strength to stop her from jumping on them.

When my mother died we gave Sniffy to the owner of a horse riding school in the country where she ducked and dived in between the horses legs. Gareth was in and out of clinics and hospitals, Dad didn't have the time to look after her, and there was nowhere else for her to go.

After subsequent overdoses he would sometimes have a bout in what Callum, Gareth and I came to call the nuthouse. These periods would vary in length depending on the possible physical implications of the overdose. If there could have been permanent damage, he would have to spend longer in hospital because his action was deemed more sectionable. Different levels of destruction and seriousness of intent commanded the duration and nature of his stay, whether he could come and go freely, whether he could only leave the hospital during set times, whether he could have visitors, whether he was persuaded to be a voluntary patient, or if he was sectioned. If he tried to or succeeded in absconding from the hospital for any length of time, on his return he would have to spend more time confined to the ward. The memory of these periods have blurred into one long institutionalized existence so that I do not know how much of his life he spent within the walls of clinical officialdom, nor do I know how much of it he spent at home. It seemed as though he was often either in hospital or attending it for treatment. And if he wasn't at the Royal Free he was attending other clinics.

I don't remember when he was first committed. I do remember going to the hospital soon after one overdose, maybe it was his third or fourth, and he was ordering us to get him out of there because he was under a section. Can you imagine entering a psychiatric ward and knowing you have to stay there?

How will a depressed or suicidal person fare better when they are faced with walls that close in upon them? The bright fluorescent lights dry eyes and beat upon your head whether or not you're ill. Beds, with only a curtain around them for privacy, are far from the sanctuary they could be – at any moment someone might pop a head round to check up on you. No place for the mind to rest in peace. And anyone can have access to your few belongings any time you're not there to protect the MDF cupboard that stands next to your bed. The lino floors get mopped with disinfectant every day, they shine as you intrude upon the sameness, they mock you because you don't really want to be there. They glare at you as you wander, searching for your sibling. And they carry the hospital smell, the one which anchors itself right there in the plastic of those floors.

In the dining room there was a choice between two dishes for dinner. The obligatory mushy peas and school dinner desserts, regressing patients to childhood days spent in another institution. Feed them as though they are children and maybe they'll act like them. The over-brewed tea after dinner, with bits of scum that float on top because it's been hanging around for too long. That rough toilet paper that is significantly cheaper than the soft stuff which would greatly eat into the NHS budget, and so must be used, but really serves to tell patients where they are when the roughness scratches their arses, as if they could forget. There was the kitchen, where they were free to make tea and coffee, but not much else. Other patients wandered around, and they, at first, seemed odd to Gareth because he thought he didn't belong there.

'Get me out of here,' he said when we went to visit him after that overdose. He sat in a chair in the day room. Other patients busied themselves around him, going about their daily habits; watching telly, eating, and chatting to each other or themselves. Or sitting in silence with eyes on Gareth because he looked as though he might be worth a little entertainment, especially as we were there to add to the show.

'But it might help you to be here for a little while,' I ventured, feeling guilty for the betrayal, for the treacherous low-down slimy words that could only scorn him in that frame of mind. He didn't alter his stare. Straight ahead, he fixed onto anything that wasn't us. And, ashamedly, I was thinking I didn't want him at home because things were easier, quieter, more bearable, when he wasn't there. I tried to reason with him because I wanted him to stay in hospital.

It was clear that none of us knew what to do with him when he was home and no one gave us advice. I had no idea what would be best for him even as I suggested that maybe he should give it a go. Not that we had the power to get him out anyway, he was sectioned and there was nothing we could do about it.

Gareth didn't see it that way. He seemed to think, in these irregular circumstances, that because we'd called the ambulance we were at fault. We put him there so it was down to us to get him out. I have often wondered how he would have behaved had it been one of us who'd lost it now and then, if it had been one of us who ended up in that ward. It didn't occur to me to question whether that hospital was good or bad for him. That hospital meant that he wasn't with us and Mum wasn't as wrecked. I didn't want to be in the same house with him anymore.

'I don't give a fucking fuck. I'm not going to stay here.'

Whatever Gareth was, he wasn't daft. It might have been easier to tell him what was right for him, not that anyone claimed to know, if he had been. He was suicidal but he wasn't nuts. Whatever that random distinction between nuts and non-nuts is, he wasn't nuts, he was just impossible. It was hard to know what to do with impossible. So we left him there, that time in the day room, staring through us because he didn't want us to exist.

Other times we would walk away as he lay on his bed, with the rumpled white sheets and blanket, and the curtain drawn around his portion of space as the only pretence of architectural privacy. Down in the lift one more time. Leaving the face that thinks it has been deceived and wants to reject you because you've left him there, but needs you to come back because so little exists in that world. The thick varnish of numbness that glazed me stubbornly stuck to my skin each time he was difficult to deal with. I had a lack of tears for his sadness because it had all, at some point, become normal. Overdoses and hospitalization is what I came to expect from him. If it had come out of the blue, maybe I would have tried more, fought more. But this was how Gareth was since I was small, so I didn't fight. Instead I visited and humoured.

On another section, after a different overdose, he was followed everywhere as if he were a prisoner. Every single one of his innocent or guilty gestures was watched. It was necessary to keep him alive. He was walked to the toilet where the nurse would wait outside, or to the payphone stuck on the wall. If you weren't mad already it could drive you mad; being tailed, having someone attached to your heels, registering your every move.

One time, when he came out of intensive care, he was given his own room in the ward. He had space; he didn't have other patients surrounding him as the dark thoughts flooded his beautiful, depressed, lonely mind. He had a little privacy, though he was too drugged up to realize it.

I took the bath I was running when the police had rung the doorbell. No death changes dirt. The water rose to cover my skin as I lowered myself into the white oval. It had chilled so I turned on the hot tap with my foot. Water is loved by my brothers and I, and my mother's favourite sound was the pouring of tea from a pot, the current of the infused water. Gareth adored the patter of rain against a window. He liked to get caught in the rain – perhaps it awoke his senses to nature existing beyond his gloom. Callum reveres the sea for its power to carry him on its waves. I feel alive when swimming in calm blue salty waters.

I found myself curling into the foetal position. The water sloshed over my face – I stayed under for as long as I could without breath. Bathing made me think of the foetus in a womb surrounded by fluids. How Gareth was once in Mum.

When Gareth was living with my father and I, after our mother had left the family home, he would have these incredibly long baths, sometimes for several hours. Self-imposed hydrotherapy. When I returned from school in the afternoon he would be behind the locked bathroom door soaking himself, turning his skin into a shrivelled, wrinkly and newborn-looking substance. He brought his stereo into the bathroom and listened to the radio whilst bathing. It's a wonder he didn't electrocute himself – then again, maybe that was the plan. By the time he'd finished, the bathroom looked like a locker-room after a prize fight. Screwed up and soaked through towels were strewn on the floor, the soap too was left on the floor where it fell, waiting for someone to slip on it, and puddles of water littered the floor. Somehow, Gareth would make a mess whether he was taking a bath, cooking a meal, or even drinking an innocent cup of tea.

Gareth's tea drinking was as novel as his wit. He drank tea in the same way great rice eaters eat rice. He held the cup up to his mouth, drew it in close to his chin, and with a teaspoon he would make the short journey from cup to mouth with spoon after spoon of sickly sweet tea. He would consume the whole cup in this way and did so with thirsty speed. To unintentionally mark the zone of his tea ceremony, he would, without fail, fling half of the liquid around his sitting body as if throwing salt over the shoulder.

I lay in the bath with the knowledge that I had to tell my father his son had just committed suicide. When I had told him about my mother's death it was on the telephone; this would be in person. I had to while away the hours until he came home. I almost thought more about how to tell him than I did about the death of my brother. The elusive quality of time disappears in a crisis, the need to speed up events is impossible and desperate. How could I know when he did not, he must come home and know. I tried to smoke a cigarette, but I couldn't. I had given up in India, deterred by Indian tobacco. The authentic white stick so craved for was disgusting.

I was thinking about how noisy Gareth was, and how now he would be silent.

When we were at school he played the trumpet. Blew that bashed brass horn and filled the house with discordant noise. Swerving around doors, through walls and floors, the notes hit out with a lack of elegance. He looked dead serious as he puffed away, and his cheeks, either side of his rounded mouth and the instrument, would fill up with air nearly to bursting point in order to make more sounds that didn't seem pleased to have been made. The vibrations wandered even when doors were shut. He persevered, he practised and he played, and it suited him. He gave the trumpet to me once, as if daring me to compete. If I'd been able to play it I would have got a thump. But I couldn't even get enough breath to squeak out one note.

After a few hours Dad came home, and I realized how devastating the thing that he didn't yet know was. One second he was without knowing, the next his mind would be precarious, raging, desolate. He took off his coat and put down his briefcase and the manuscripts he was holding – he is a literary agent. We stood in the middle of his living room. As always he stood tall, upright, head held high. I said that he might want to sit down, as if such preparation could soften the facts. He remained standing. I rarely told him things of great significance, so he knew that because we were alone in a room facing each other, something was very wrong. I unhesitatingly blurted out what his son had done.

'Gareth has killed himself.'

'You're joking,' he replied.

He stood like a statue, in shock. I put my arms around him. There he was with his arms by his sides, frozen. Ice.

'Poor Gareth,' he said to me. I looked him in the eye and replied, 'Poor you.'

'Poor you,' he repeated, and let out a half-hearted laugh. Admission of irretrievable devastation is not part of our father's make-up. Before the night was over he was claiming Gareth's suicide was inevitable, that it was just a matter of time. Inevitability does, after all, play some kind of role in justifying the unbearable.

21

Accusation, too, played a role. 'I knew that bloody hospital shouldn't have let him out.'

They should have kept him in a clinical cage forever, forcibly stopping the miserable being from putting himself down.

Strangely the evening progressed. Darkness came, and we needed food. We decided to have an Indian takeaway, but neither of us set off to get it. He sat in the corner of the room in his chair by the window. For him it was advantageous because he could look out of the window rather than focus on me. With blame wedged in his intonation he started talking.

'Gareth has always been difficult. He was always breaking things in the house. Always causing chaos.'

Minutes later he was trying to hold back the tears.

As children, out of the three of us, it was probably me that spent the most time with Dad.

Often I would hang around in his study at home whilst he was working. I remember his typewriter. My father made it click with as much speed as the driver of a racing car. He typed away with only two fingers, nimbly they skitted and pressed. The rat-a-tat-tat, the tune the letters played. I would pretend I could type as fast as he even before I could spell, didn't know the words and tapped anyway. Haste was the order of the day in his study so I skipped my fingers across the lettered pads. A military of Ks and Ds lined up, imprinted themselves upon the perfect bleached paper. And at the end of each line, the satisfying ding.

Then he got a new typewriter, an electric one with red lights that flashed on and off like beacons announcing themselves. This was a broader creature. Not so black, not so metallic. I didn't like the look of it much. But this one could zoom. This one didn't get stuck. And it could cleverly undo. But best of all, he gave me the old one zipped up in its case and upon it I played.

He worked hard, for years he had two jobs, a literary agent by day and a theatre critic by night. Although he didn't spend that much time at home, he was a sustaining presence to me. Every morning he'd wake me up before school and make my breakfast. One phase was dominated by egg and soldiers. He would cook the egg to perfection. The white had to be perfectly firm, the yolk runny, it mustn't have the chance to harden into a pale crumbling yellow. He'd smash the egg with a teaspoon to stop it cooking further once it was on the table, then I'd slice into the curved summit and remove the top as though it were a lid. The soldiers were covered in chunks of salty butter, still hard from the fridge: he didn't battle with it for slivers that would melt into the thickly cut toast. Too rich for me, I'd scrape the butter away before dipping the edible army. After the egg era came Rice Krispies. He'd bring them to me in bed when he woke me, drenched in milk. I preferred milk from a newly opened bottle because I wanted the cream that sat beneath the foil top. I liked the way the cereal made the milk sugary. A sweetness that increased as you got closer to the bottom of the bowl of puffed rice.

In the bathroom once, as we were both cleaning our teeth, before Dad went to work and I went to school, he yawned, and then I yawned. We started laughing, perhaps yawns were contagious. We decided to test our hypothesis on my mother at breakfast. He and I sat there exaggeratedly feigning yawns, trying not to giggle, to see if she would succumb. She didn't, and merely looked at us as though we were mad.

When he was a theatre critic, he often took me with him to shows. I didn't really care what we were seeing, I revelled in the whole outing – the dressing up, the theatre's architecture, the set design, the costumes and the drama.

Afterwards he would sometimes take me to the Garrick Club for dinner which I found a slightly odd experience, probably because young girls, like grown women, weren't allowed in certain rooms which, even as a child, struck me as absurd. The first time I went Mum had told me that I must have a look at the Ladies. There were pale frills, lace, soft cushions, antique hairbrushes, a marble fireplace and Victorian prints on the walls. It seemed to me that the bathroom was that fancy in the hope that women would spend more of their time there than with their men, who were, no doubt, in the rooms where no women were allowed. Once, a vote was taken to decide if the no women restrictions should be maintained. My father voted to get the women in, but the majority opted to uphold the separation of the sexes.

The restaurant was another issue. Everything on the menu was too rich for me so Dad would ask the waiter if I could have chips. The chef would come out and have a word with me to check that was sufficient and then I would be presented with a plate of pristine chips. I would then request tomato ketchup, which drove my father crazy.

'You can't have ketchup in the Garrick. It's bad enough that you're having chips!'

'I can't have chips without ketchup.'

And then we would eat, he annoyed that I was being what he thought common in an uncommon place, in the high-ceilinged splendour of the Garrick. Once the chef made me a pizza, my father was dismayed. 'This is the first and last time a pizza will be eaten in the Garrick.' It was a world away from life with Gareth.

Night followed day and day followed night. I awoke to the brutal conscious recollection that Gareth was dead.

We didn't know where Callum was. For the second time he wasn't to be found when one of us had died. Far away from the end of a phone, an unknowing fugitive. Once again the police were looking for him, trying to find him through his car registration, to tell him to contact us. He would have known, like me, what it was about if the police approached him. He called us on the second day of our knowing. He was surfing in Cornwall, just as he had been when our mother died. My father told him that his brother had committed suicide. I spoke to him afterwards.

'If he wasn't dead I'd kill him. What a bloody idiot.'

Gareth liked to go to the cinema. It contributed to the escapist trail. If you can't disappear through death, disappear into the counterfeit worlds of others. Callum and I would often go with him. He would drive everyone in the auditorium to distraction with his vocal reactions. If the film made him jump, or had him on the edge of his seat, he would shout out, 'Fuck! Fucking hell. Did you see that?' The audience would turn in dismay and tut, but would refrain from saying anything that resembled an audible complaint. Gareth was oblivious to his abuse of cinema etiquette and would continue his lively interruptions throughout the film.

The three of us took our little half-sister to see *Aladdin*. Gareth was her joker and her clown, he adored her. He held her high on his shoulders as we walked to the cinema, and she screamed and giggled in one breath. When he took her down she screamed even harder as her feet touched the ground and refused to walk another step. She went on a walking strike and sat on the pavement in protest, the only remedy was to put her right back on Gareth's shoulders where she could pull his hair and stick her fingers in his ears.

At the cinema we bought the biggest box of popcorn to share. Lucy was tiny in her plush velvet seat, and placed on her lap the huge box came up to her chin, she only had to draw her chin in and lower her mouth to reach the corn. With her hands holding the box, she munched away while her eyes locked on the big screen to be mesmerized by the exoticism of *Aladdin*. There we were, four of us sitting in a row, three protecting one. But none of us could shield the one who really needed a sanctuary.

Once he tried to jump off the roof of the Swiss Cottage cinema. He got drunk, climbed up the stairs of the fire exit and drank more to give himself the courage to make the leap. Instead, he passed out. He was found up there by the police. Someone must have seen him walk up the stairs and reported it.

Callum, Gareth and I laughing together felt like home, like brandy warming from the inside out. Walking between my two brothers, their blood was like pillars either side of me. Gareth was taller and broader than Callum, whose compact athletic physique came from canoeing, basketball, snowboarding and surfing. All three of us grew late and when we did have our growth spurts we shot up quickly. Gareth, who had said he felt like a dwarf, passed six feet. When his laughing stopped we thought we had gone backwards. Wanting to keep someone alive and hiding potential weapons is one thing, cheering up a depressive is another challenge altogether. A good day or night was considered an achievement.

Chapter Two

Gareth very nearly died in the suicide attempt he made about a year before his death. He had been hoarding his daily medication. Life-saving, life-destroying pills, popped in the mouth and out the mouth, just as soon as he'd walked away from the little room where medication was dished out. Stored up as if preparing for hibernation. A small mountain of pills saved and saved until there were enough. Weeks of medication were swallowed as if they were one dose. One fatal dose. But he was too strong.

My father and I went together to see him in hospital. In casualty, lying on a bed and punctured by tubes, his liver corroded, his heart still beating. A grey-white body, a sheet drawn up over his chest. The doctor told us that half of those malignant little white pills could have killed him. His body so resilient – up to a point. The doctor said that Gareth might have a heart attack within the next three days or he may have brain damage.

Lying there, he already looked dead. Would he get up like the speared bull in the ring? Coloured ribbons knifed into the animal's flesh marking his imminent fall. The bigger the knife, the more elaborate the ribbon on its end. The bull thunders to the ground, blood pouring from his mouth and wounds, one leg buckles, then another, then he collapses. The crowd cheers. The stubborn fearless ones struggle to stand for one last act of the fight, rising only to be struck once more.

Unconscious, he looked peaceful, liberated from anger and fear. Seeing him like this evoked a startling longing to let him go. I believed he should not be roused. Draped in white sheets in the midst of casualty confusion, he should be allowed to flee. Not pumped out, not brought back from his success and our defeat. Doctors around him ran here and there, attending to the next crisis now that he was all tubed up.

As my father and I walked down Pond Street, I said, as much to myself as to him, 'I wish they'd just let him go.'

'Don't be so bloody stupid,' he replied. He couldn't let him leave. We kept walking at a pace determined by him. Dad is a fast walker, his stride is never compromised.

That night, a friend of my brothers and I sat on her bed, with candles burning, and prayed that he might take flight. That was his time, we believed, because we were scared his life might be harder if he were brain damaged. Then he wouldn't even have the choice of wanting or not wanting to live.

I thought about how it might be if he were gone, how his life would no longer be miserable, how it would no longer be at all. How I would be strong because that was what he truly wanted. But it was bullshit. There was no rationale. I needed him, wanted to see his face, not just envision it from time to time. Maybe I allowed his suicide because I thought those thoughts. Maybe I made it easier for him to go. It's hard not to think that.

The next night I went to the hospital alone. Freshly pumped out, Gareth had been moved to a floor higher up. It was a whole new experience. I didn't automatically go up to his second home in that familiar ward, I had to enquire at reception to find out where he was.

His new and temporary abode was restful and quiet in contrast to the psychiatric ward. It was a quiet I had not known before. A calming nurse with bright orange hair, one who surprised me with his gentleness, took my name and told me that Gareth remained unconscious. He walked with me to Gareth's bed. Before he left he asked if I needed anything – a nicety that could push one over the edge. There he lay, looking, as always, much less derelict when asleep. We were surrounded by windows and it was dark outside. The view was free of reflections because the ward's lighting was dimmed while patients slept or were unconscious. I saw stars sparkling and trees on Hampstead Heath. It was like no other moment I had had in that hospital, and it was even more unusual to experience such tranquillity with him, with his unconscious body near me.

Despite the peace I felt, outside there was a storm. It pulsated, wrenched leaves from trees and made music with the swaying branches. It struck me how phenomenal it is that nature's forces don't always destroy. Most trees stay upright and rooted, and most branches stay attached. It felt as though the storm washed away the misery, stripped it, poured away the darkness as the rain ran down a road, a drain, flowed down the hill.

I thought he would die then. But he came back.

The three danger days went by without Gareth suffering a heart attack and he was moved back to his old ward in the psychiatric unit. Now it was brain damage or a full recovery. I walked through the corridors of the clinical route. More sensitive than usual, having come close to losing my brother, I was delicate and could be easily broken. As I passed through the unlocked doors, one of the nurses approached me before I reached Gareth's room.

'Who are you, and where do you think you're going?' Aggression was in his scratchy tone.

'To see my brother, Gareth.'

'Well you can't just walk in here like that, with that attitude.'

I was as tall as him and reached his height.

'I don't have an attitude. I just want to see Gareth.'

He said nothing to me, just glared an ugly glare.

I wondered how such figures weaselled their way into these positions, where they have power to inflict further distress on the vulnerable.

As he recovered from this overdose Gareth was stalked by the dark corners of his mind. Flitting between fairy-tale visions and more sinister fantasises, he saw magic or disaster. Searing his soul were ravaged monster–ghosts. They bided their time, then pounced to quench their thirst and sate their hunger, just as he thought they were leaving. A sad, long-lost soul was cloaked by Gareth's great, tired body.

He saw monsters coming to get him, grabbed me by the arm and tried to run. When I told him nothing was coming he became screamingly angry.

'They're there for fuck's sake, come on, we've got to go, run! Are you fucking blind!'

The nurse helped me get him back into bed, his eyes scanned the room for horrors and, finding none, he became passive. As I sat by his bed with tears running down my cheeks, he saw my mascara-covered lashes as spider legs. Truly, spiders were crawling into my eyes. Then the lashes became softer in his sight, less creepy creatures, and he carefully stroked them. My brother's fingers were gentle over my face. Looking intently, this Alice in Wonderland vision led him to a feast for his eyes. He did not see me or his usual feared reality so I could cry freely. Another's upset in his non-hallucinogenic state would have been too much for him to bear. There would have been too many questions to answer that were not about him and his illness. Too many external forces to make it all much, much worse. Chemicals acted like muslin between us, and I cried silently, unwatched, unquestioned.

Slowly, Gareth retreated from that toxic fantasy. He came back in just a few days. He sat up in bed.

'How do you feel?' I asked.

'Like shit. I nearly did it though. My hand's buggered, it fell onto the radiator when I conked out.' It was swollen, puffed up to twice the size of his other hand. Because he had been out of it he didn't know he was burning, boiling his skin until a blister inches long took hold. 'I can't move my fingers. They're going to stick some voltage through it today to sort it out.'

We talked but it was strange. His words were all mixed up, his vocabulary had descended into mild revolution. When he responded to my mundane chat he delivered misplaced jargon in amongst what he wanted to say. I kept going, mostly I knew what he meant and I didn't want to enhance his paranoia or belittle him by pointing out his irrelevant mistakes. Before me was someone who thought he knew what he had said.

We walked out of the ward – he had permission because it was for further treatment. We went down a couple of floors to where the voltage was. Gareth was slightly unstable, his co-ordination was affected by the overdose, he looked drunk and people stared. The doctor he saw was a lively man. I wondered if he knew Gareth's background and was trying to perk him up. Gareth sat in a chair that looked like it belonged in a barber's shop. It was in the middle of the room. Thoughts of electroconvulsive therapy crept into my head along with tales of death by electrocution. I feared for what could have happened to him in decades and centuries gone by. Worse, for what treatment could happen still. He was there to have the nerves in his hand jump-started. Others have their minds blasted.

Ugo Cerletti, a professor of psychiatry in Rome, developed Electroconvulsive Therapy (ECT). He conducted his first experiments on dogs, then on pigs in slaughterhouses. In 1938 the treatment was administered on human subjects. ECT spread rapidly within the world of psychiatry and became a major treatment for schizophrenia and depression during the next two decades. Early in the 1940s it was introduced to England and soon became widely used throughout the country. Prior to muscle-relaxant drugs, patients were held down by several nurses as the shocks caused their bodies to spasm and convulse. Fractures to the spine and limbs were not uncommon. A gag was placed in the patient's mouth to prevent him or her biting their tongue. These days, the patient is put to sleep with a short-acting sedative and a drug is administered to temporarily paralyse the muscles so they do not contract during the treatment and cause fractures. An electrode is applied to each temple. A small current is passed through the brain, activating a seizure. The seizure must last for at least thirty seconds for it to be clinically effective. Heart rhythm disturbances are common throughout the procedure, as is temporary, but occasionally permanent, memory loss.

In 1935 a Portuguese neurosurgeon, Dr Antonio Egas Moniz, developed the lobotomy and experimented on those deemed to be on the fringes of society, provided by the Portuguese government. He believed he had found an appropriate treatment to control schizophrenics, alcoholics, homosexuals and, potentially, political dissidents. In 1949 he received a Nobel Prize for refining the irreversible lobotomy technique to be used in cases of psychosis or severe depression. In the 1940s and 1950s an estimated 50,000 lobotomies were performed worldwide – 15,000 of which were carried out in England.

The doctor dragged over to the chair a trolley laden with boxes and wires. He attached the wires to Gareth's puffed hand. He joked about the voltage, 'We won't fry you this time!' Electricity strived to harass his nerves. Gareth did not jerk or convulse, he felt tingling and tried to twiddle his fingers to see if the zap had worked.

'You'll be needing more sparks in a few days.'

Gareth was further depressed by his damaged hand. The one thing he did want to do in life was compose music, eventually, he hoped, for films. When he was out of hospital he spent his days experimenting on keyboards he had accumulated since his teenage years. He was exhilarated by the accuracy of the instrumental sounds they mimicked. The first thing he would do when I visited him at his flat was play to me new sounds he had discovered buried in his machines. 'Listen to this.' And before allowing it to finish he would start playing the next one, 'and this.' Most of what he composed remained unfinished, but he did complete some pieces. They were either comical clinkings and clangings, music to accompany a contemporary Buster Keaton, or they were impassioned, peaking in emotive crescendos. If his hand was permanently damaged, one of the few things he enjoyed would be gone.

His earlier overdoses weren't quite so dramatic. Though I don't know how the first one unfolded. My mother must have found him. Did she go upstairs and wake him in the morning and he told her what he'd done? Did she have to bring him round from a drowsy state? Or did he come and tell her?

Once, after Gareth had overdosed he threw up on the stairs as he was coming down from his bedroom. I heard him as he started to be sick, I went to him and he stood there up above me, hunched, his head hanging low, shoulders raised up and leaning forward in a gesture of pointless self protection.

I asked the obvious question, 'Have you taken something?'

'Yes.'

'How many?'

'Nearly the whole bottle.'

With a calmness worthy of my mother, I went to Dad and asked him to call an ambulance while I sat with Gareth.

When the ambulance came, we accompanied Gareth outside and helped him into it. Afterwards I went up into his bedroom, where I saw the empty pill bottle. I ran down the stairs, out into the street and gave the paramedics the bottle. Gareth, still conscious, though barely, sat wrapped in a blanket.

We lived in such a cosy cul-de-sac, cosy enough that we would leave our side door unlocked, as other families in the street did, so that we children could come and go from different houses at whim. The monstrous white ambulance was an overt intrusion. It looked as though it would have been too big to fit in the street but, nevertheless, it had manoeuvred its way up it. They closed the hefty back doors and I watched the ambulance drive – it moved away slowly down the slight hill. The light glowed within it, and I could guess what they would be doing to him. Asking him questions, how many pills, how long ago had he taken them, and so forth. They would take his blood pressure, check his pulse, and ensure that he wasn't about to die there and then. Consciousness was always a good sign. It couldn't be all that bad if he was still awake.

There was a sinking feeling in my stomach as I watched it leave. Another one, he'd placed another vote to end it all. And I felt a strange, remarkable peace – in that instant there is no waiting because it has happened. The darkness was a shield, to have him put into an ambulance in the glaring daylight would have been too harsh. With the night came gentleness. Standing in the dark there is less to see.

In the houses on either side of the street other families went about their business.

At one quite desperate point, more desperate than the others, Gareth went through a phase of giving up on the common overdose as his method of self-destruction and came up with all sorts of other ideas. Absurdly, when he spoke openly of his newly formulated plans for his impending death, it didn't strike us hard – in fact, it struck us less and less each time. After a while you got used to it and it would go over your head because you'd heard it all before and because it was too difficult to hear again. Something inside would shut down. There was excitement in his face when he spoke of these plans. He acted as though he were an inventor who had come across some mesmerizing new discovery, and the frequency with which he made these statements had the effect of making it seem like we were discussing how you might go about cooking a certain dish or solve a certain mechanical problem. No doubt this was the result of having his behaviour as part of our day-to-day lives for years.

All the things he had been getting up to only seemed out of the ordinary when he died. Suddenly there wasn't the constant threat of him being whisked off to casualty, nor of us rushing there to find out about the latest attempt. To know that there would be no more visits to see him in hospital, that's what was strange. What was supposedly normal had become corrupted years before, and Gareth being suicidal had become our normality.

The highlight of Gareth's disjointed thoughts was his theoretical ingenuity with an air pump, used to filter the water in fish tanks. Because overdosing on painkillers and anti-depressants and anything else he could get his hands on hadn't worked, Gareth came up with what he thought was a faultless plan. He wanted Callum or I to bring him an air pump and a plastic tube. Gareth thought he could cut himself, insert the tube into one of his arteries, attach the pump, turn it on and wait for his blood to be pumped out of him. It was a preposterous idea – that plan was fatally flawed from the outset. As Callum said, 'How much power did he think those pumps had?'

We didn't bring him the pump or tube and he didn't manage to get hold of either from anyone else. Disappointed, he decided to cut himself anyway. He went into the bathroom on his ward and cut himself on his neck in an attempt to get one of the main arteries. His blood sprayed the walls of the bathroom and he passed out. Horizontal, the red liquid of life didn't leak away. When I arrived in hospital to see him after this episode, I paid a visit to the same toilet and although the floor had been cleaned, I found splattered traces of his blood still on the walls. At first I thought it was disgraceful. Why hadn't the cleaners cleaned up his blood thoroughly? Then I thought, who the hell would want to clean up the blood of a suicidal stranger?

A wound was left where blood had spurted forth, a beige skinny scar that sat on his neck as if glued to it, reminding the skin of its damage, of the war waged against it. It didn't fit with the rest of his colour. It stood out as the burns on his hand and forearm had for ages after he passed out with his arm on the radiator. The signs of the fights the body has had with its owner.

Another bright idea of Gareth's was heroin. Whilst in hospital he asked Callum if he could get him a lethal dose of the stuff, which Callum refused to do. Apart from anything else, he didn't plan on being arrested as an accessory as well as ending up with a dead brother. So Gareth asked me, and laid the guilt on thick and fast. Who did I think I was to not help him when I couldn't conceive for one second how miserable and desperate he was? By not doing what he asked I was prolonging his agony. He said it was easy for me to say no, because I wasn't in his position.

When the hospital staff took away his belt and razors while he was on a section after a suicide attempt, he asked me to get him more razors. He expected me to trust him, to be a partner in his crime. He almost assumed I was, and that I undoubtedly should be compliant in his attempts. That, I was there to help him because I was his sister.

'Look, I need a shave,' he asserted when I said I didn't think I should bring him razors.

What could I say?

'You're not going to do anything with them are you?' Guilty for asking, like I was breaching the trust he thought was there, but couldn't be because of all the other attempts.

'Look at my face will you. I need a fucking shave.' I didn't bring them. I pretended to forget, like a child who forgets to clean their teeth at night. But like the aspirin that was hidden from him, he got hold of them from elsewhere. It is impossible to keep dangerous objects away from someone who wants to die. They'll find what they want somehow. Nevertheless, he did use them for shaving and shaving only.

Soon after he phoned me up in tears. He said he was in unbearable physical pain but the doctors were refusing to give him any more painkillers. He asked if I could buy him the most potent over-the-counter drugs I could find and bring them to the hospital as soon as possible. He wanted two packets and he promised he wouldn't overdose. So why two packets? To trust or not to trust. I brought them to him, gave him the suggested dose, kept the rest and said I'd come back later to give him more.

At the time he wasn't allowed out of hospital unless he was accompanied. I'd pick him up and we'd go for a walk, to the cinema, or to the coffee shop in South End Green he liked, where he'd eat several cream cakes, we'd have tea and chat like any other brother and sister. Then when it came to taking him back he'd ask if he could walk the last part without me simply because he wanted to have a few minutes on his own as he could never be completely alone in hospital. I took risks. I did things that I shouldn't have, but I was so entwined with his appeals for sympathy, even though he was on a section, I relented more often than was safe. Each time he promised me he would go back, and every time he did.

It was a double act. He would consistently tell anyone who would listen that he wanted to die and would give frequent demonstrations of his sincerity. Then he would assume we trusted him enough to give him potentially lethal items and to leave him alone. We were, on some level, supposed to have faith that he wouldn't use us to succeed in his cause. We were mental pawns, moved and messed around. He had us bound. There wasn't trust between us because he was constantly threatening to disappear. But the alternative threat was that he would disappear from us if we didn't help. Appeasing him in either scenario would result in loss. If I didn't occasionally go along with Gareth's requests to have time alone or buy him painkillers, he would have cut me off like he cut off anyone who didn't do what he wanted. You didn't have to do everything for him, he wasn't totally unreasonable, but you did have to go so far, you did have to engage in a little voluntary naivety.

It was a ludicrous situation allayed by nothing, until his death, and then I saw the madness of it all. The ridiculous part is that when he was alive I thought I was supporting him, and I thought I was doing it from a cool distance. I didn't realize he'd had me very much involved in the tricks he and his wilful mind played. Only when he was gone did I learn he'd had me in his clutches. Although, ultimately, he never did use us, he found other ways.

Once, the police turned up at Gareth's flat to ask Callum, who was staying there while Gareth was in hospital, if he knew where his younger brother was. Gareth hadn't returned to the hospital at his allotted time, so they had alerted the local constabulary, and asked the police to go to the flat. Callum hadn't seen him nor known he was missing. The policeman asked him to call the hospital if he heard any news. Likewise, Callum asked him to come back and let him know if Gareth turned up, as Gareth deliberately hadn't had a phone installed so he couldn't be reached. The policeman agreed.

Callum heard nothing for several hours and continued to wait for the policeman to return. Meanwhile, a friend he'd arranged to meet waited for him in a pub in Camden Town all evening. But, fretting, he remained in the flat. It was the first time he thought Gareth had really gone and done it, not least because he'd been telling everyone for a while that it was time to do it again. Callum was having all kinds of visions, of his brother dead or lying unconscious, having taken an overdose and gone somewhere for the poison to kick in. When handed the beginning of the scenario – police come to discuss your brother's disappearance – it's not hard to finish it for yourself. Any number of things could have happened and Callum has a good imagination. A few hours later, having heard nothing from the police, he called the hospital from a phone box to find out if there was any news. He was told Gareth had walked into the ward, cool as a cucumber, having lost track of time. He hadn't run away at all. He'd got incredibly drunk with a friend and forgotten to return to hospital. On realizing the hour the friend took him back. He'd no intention of killing himself that night. First, Callum was livid with the police for not coming back and telling him. And second, with Gareth.

When they next met Callum told Gareth he cared about him and didn't want him to die, that Gareth had put him in the situation where he thought he'd done it. He apologized, but in true Gareth style he was shocked the incident had caused such a reaction. He acted as though Callum was a fool for worrying about it. He didn't get it. Callum had been the one stuck waiting. Some of our thoughts were always about waiting, about the possibility, about what he had taken so much time and energy to instil into our heads. He may have thought we didn't listen but we had, and it had sunk in. He spoke about dying, then when he saw our fear because we believed him, he tried to downplay it, made out that we were hysterical for responding. He wanted suicide without the trouble of anyone missing him. He didn't seem to understand the impact it would have. He didn't seem to know we didn't want him to die. That we wanted him to live.

Shortly after that incident they had a huge row. Callum was cooking a Vietnamese meal in Gareth's flat for the two of them. Gareth liked to spend his time out of hospital in his flat – he viewed it as his sanctuary. A housing association had found it for him when my father decided Gareth could no longer live at home without harming us. He must have been eighteen when he moved out. Despite his months of refusing to leave the family house, when he did eventually go, he quickly came to cherish having his own space. In the summer we used to eat sitting on the window ledge overlooking the street, with a view of Primrose Hill. That evening as they ate, perched half inside and half outside, Gareth started the all too familiar rant about how he wanted to kill himself and how he might go about it. This time, however, the ever-patient Callum had had enough and challenged his behaviour. Did he really want to die or was he playing with fire?

Someone who genuinely planned to die, Callum suggested, could discard their life in many daredevil ways. It couldn't be that hard to kill yourself. If you really wanted to die, what would stop you from succeeding? The suicidal person could become a real-life stunt man or woman if they were devoid of self-preservation. Callum imagined Gareth could climb cliff faces no person respectful of life would, or dare to swim in seas which notoriously crushed those brave enough to try and negotiate their force, or take tempting drugs with the assurance that the outcome was irrelevant. If you plan to die, why not make it an adventure? What a waste it would be to die by your own hand and not do so with some flair.

The relentless verbal threats knifed the blood between two brothers. Callum was pushed to his limit, Gareth had goaded him into saying how easy it could be. If he was going to do it, Callum couldn't stop it. Nobody could.

'I'm fed up of hearing about it, of you going on about it. If you're going to do it, just do it, but stop fucking talking about it.'

'It's not as simple as that,' Gareth replied to such testing logic. He spoke of the sheer terror of looking down at concrete from the top of high buildings and the fear of jumping in front of a train and of the consequences if it went wrong. What if he didn't die and instead became more damaged?

Callum tried to tell him it was very painful to hear about it all the time.

Gareth replied, 'You don't know how hard it is.'

'It's not that hard. Just go to the top of the Royal Free and jump out the window.'

'It's so smooth when you look down,' Gareth replied, making little sense to Callum. Too smooth and hard a surface to fall upon, was that it? Too smooth to have your perfect limbs crash upon it? Too impossible to turn back, unlike the ambiguous outcome of overdosing on prescription drugs. He opted for the unreliable, dormant way. Taking sweet pills that enticed the long sleep.

Callum kept going. 'Take your pills, but don't come back to the flat which is the first place everyone will come to look for you.'

'But it's comfortable here,' said the one that wanted to die. Who wouldn't want to be comfortable in their last moments?

'Run away from the hospital, get on the tube, go to the end of the line where they won't find you, walk off down a country road and take your pills.'

'People will see me lying in the road.'

'Don't lie in the road. Lie in a ditch where no one will see you. '

'I'll get cold.'

'You're telling me that your life is so bad that you want to end it, but not if it involves getting a bit chilly. Take a fucking blanket.'

Gareth was shocked that Callum was so fervently angry with him because he never had been before. Normally he was calm and patient with everyone, including Gareth. I was the one who had the reputation for having a temper that would snap quickly, easily and loudly. My father once said I was like a piece of china waiting to break everyday. Though I never broke with Gareth because of the unknown outcome. Unable to hear any more, Gareth said he had to return to the Royal Free because his curfew was approaching.

They headed back together, Callum was responsible for making sure he arrived intact. On Adelaide Road Gareth said he needed to make a phone call. The two of them waited outside an occupied phone box. Callum noticed the derelict land the bridge they were standing on crossed over, and told Gareth that next time he took an overdose he should climb over the wall and lie there, that way no one would find him for the next few days.

Throughout Callum's monologue the man in the phone box had been looking at the two of them through the glass door. When he came out of the box he stared at Callum and couldn't scurry away quickly enough. Gareth made his call and when he'd finished Callum said, 'I'm not walking you back, go and kill yourself.'

Gareth walked off sheepishly. Callum shouted at him as he walked down the road. He wondered if Gareth might do something then, but he returned to the hospital. They didn't speak to each other for weeks after that night. Callum said he thought a lot about whether he'd been unfair and decided he hadn't been, that he'd been pushed to say those things.

Gareth called Callum one day while he was visiting at Dad's house. 'I haven't heard from you for a while.'

'I think you know why that is,' Callum replied.

'Do you want to see a film?'

Gareth believed that if someone really wanted to end it all, every cell in that body would sense it, and that person would drop dead on the spot. In some strange way he held this sentiment as a kind of assurance, as if there must be hope for him if he wasn't yet dead.

Something he used to do, which seemed to be at odds with wanting to die, was to exercise religiously every night. If you wanted to die, why would you try and make your body stronger, why would you strive for optimum health? There were the overdoses when doctors said he would have died had he not been so fit and strong. His physical strength had saved his life, he only recovered because of his almighty health. A paradox, that's what Gareth was. This keep-fit regime began long before he decided his problems were physical, so it wasn't as if he was trying to overcome the physical pain he complained of. Perhaps he was trying to find some self-esteem in the preservation of his shell.

Gareth had a set of weights in his bedroom at the top of the house. Every night we would hear him crashing them around and the whole house would feel as if it were experiencing the tremors of an earthquake. He must have dropped them often as great thuds could be heard even at the bottom of the house. It would go on for about an hour – him huffing and puffing away. Maybe a lot of frustration was being released as he pushed his adolescent body to work harder.

He was also obsessive about cleaning his teeth. Every morning and night he would spend ages doing it, preserving the shiny creamy-white enamelled shapes that sat in his mouth.

Always, even years later when the air pump experiments were being thought up, he wanted to maintain his body well. He never did let that go.

Gareth not being in the hospital when he should have been wasn't our only source of anxiety. It wasn't just a case of him not returning within the constraints of his curfew, it was also a case of keeping him there, because it wasn't hard to leave the ward at any time even if you were sectioned. A member of staff sat opposite the doors behind a glass screen and would release the lock when a visitor wanted to enter or exit the ward. Click. Yet those doors weren't always locked, and even if there was someone behind the glass it was pretty easy for patients to slink out. All they had to do was crouch down when the person on duty wasn't paying much attention. Gareth snuck out this way more than once.

The idea might have been that patients shouldn't feel locked up. But in reality, those who didn't want to be there knew full well that it wasn't hard to vacate the premises. To Callum and me the unlocked doors didn't seem so different to placing a suitable knife on a table next to a suicidal person in order to test whether or not the blade might catch their eye. At the same time we understood the complexities – hiding potential weapons of self-destruction from suicidal people is an endless task. Determined enough, they will find a way regardless. Security for the ones who want to go is a non sequitur.

Two days after Gareth's body had been found Callum returned from Newquay. Like me, he was in shock. I thought seeing him would make me believe, but he was too far gone, past the point of reaction to gruesome truths. But we were together, the two who could talk. We had been thrown together after years of being loners by the unexpected departure of the one who bore us. He didn't cling to me like a doll when she left, as I felt others had. He held me to protect me.

I remember his arrival home following Mum's death. I heard his car pull up outside our house from my bedroom and I got out of bed in the dark. He came into the house and, downstairs, my father must have told him. He came straight up to my room, wordlessly walked through the door and held me. He just held me, continued to do so, didn't stop. Both of us cried and he uttered the words, 'Are you alright?'

'Yes,' I said.

Then he got back into the car to take the friend he'd been surfing with in Newquay back home. My father was worried about him driving, and his friend said he'd take a taxi, but Callum insisted. He was practical, he kept it all together and from that moment became a figure of responsibility to me.

Our mother's death hit him days later when he was driving to Cambridge where he was studying Engineering. Randy Crawford came on to the radio, 'One Day I'll Fly Away'. That's when it got him, that's when he felt destroyed. He heard her flying away. Still he cannot hear those lyrics of leaving without being taken back to grief.

When I was six Callum rescued me from a swimming pool. We had gone on a family holiday to New York and stayed in a house outside the city belonging to some friends of Dad. They had a pool in the garden and on the first morning of waking up there I wanted to jump straight into the water. As I took my pyjamas off my mother told me to wait until someone else was ready to get into the pool with me, as I hadn't yet learnt to swim. But she was taking so long to get her swimsuit on, my brothers on the porch were just too fascinated with the free gifts you get in American breakfast cereals and my father was reading. I decided to get in by myself. Once in the pool I stood in the shallow end and announced that I would reach the other side before anyone else got in. I walked. And the water became deeper. It crawled up my body, past my shoulders, then my neck. When it got up to my chin I knew something tricky was happening, but for some reason I was convinced the water would become shallow again at any moment, just as it had become deeper. I thought if I kept moving it would recede. Suddenly I was coughing and spluttering, choking in fact, ripping my legs through the water to try and keep afloat and throwing my arms around in every direction. Through the splashes that had by now enveloped my eyes, I saw a murky Callum dive into the blue. Within seconds he had grabbed me by my arms and dragged me back to the shallow end. I coughed up water as he stood there in the pool laughing at me. 'What did you go and do that for?' he asked, seemingly oblivious to the fact that he had just stopped me swallowing half the pool's water.

'I wanted to walk from this end to that end,' I said, pointing to what I knew by then was the deep end, in stubborn disbelief at the unfair realities of swimming pools for those who cannot yet swim.

I would have another close shave with Callum nearly ten years later, when I was fifteen. We were driving in our mother's red Metro, cruising along country lanes, near to Oundle in Northamptonshire, the town our mother moved to when she left our family home. As we motored along the road Callum asked me if I would like to begin my driving lessons. I was desperate to learn to drive, I viewed it as the ultimate freedom.

He pulled over into an empty stretch at the side of the road. He explained the workings of the three pedals. Clutch, brake and accelerator. The way to remember it was as simple as ABC, but backwards. I started the car and he guided my actions with sound instruction. I was fine, I was driving and couldn't believe it. On his command I stopped the car, braking slowly and carefully. He started to explain something else to me, and I thought I'd move off whilst he was talking. I hit the accelerator and we lurched forwards. I wasn't sure what I'd done so I didn't know how to stop. I was afraid of letting everything go, to take my hands and feet off what I was controlling, albeit dangerously, in case I caused more chaos. It was Easter and Callum had been scoffing handfuls of chocolate whilst explaining the technicalities of driving to me. When I shocked the car into movement the chocolate in his hands smashed all over his face. He paused for a split second before grabbing the steering wheel from me. By the time he did grab it, we had missed a lamppost by a couple of centimetres and a ditch by not much more.

'What the fuck are you doing?' he exclaimed.

'I thought I was going to hit a different pedal,' I replied. He asked me not to tell Mum, but later, whilst she was in hospital, given that neither of us had been hurt, I thought it would make her chuckle to know, so I told her.

As we grew older, for some reason Callum was often present during my scrapes.

The first time I got blind drunk we were celebrating his twenty-first birthday. My father and I were on holiday in Greece on the island of Andros. We stayed in an old farmhouse on top of a hill. What we didn't realize until we got there was that unless you could drive, you were basically stranded halfway up a mountain with nothing and no one but each other and goats for company.

Callum and his girlfriend were spending the summer travelling around Greece and decided to spend a few days with us – thankfully, because the boredom was excruciating. One night we decided to celebrate his birthday, which had been a few days before he arrived. We had filled up the drinks cabinet with ouzo, vodka and various wines including retsina when we got to the house. We started off toasting Callum with an ouzo and then moved on to other drinks. As the night progressed I was the only one who continued to drink, but as we were having such a good time I kept on going. Suddenly I realized I was plastered, and the room was spinning around me. By this time Dad had gone upstairs to sleep and Callum was trying to keep my inebriated behaviour quiet. He kept telling me to shut up but my voice has a nasty habit of carrying at the most inopportune moments. By the time I was throwing up my father came downstairs to see what the noise was about. Poor Callum got the blame.

'What the hell have you done to her?'

My father decided I needed some fresh air and picked me up under my arms. Half dragging and half lifting he deposited me in the garden. Callum thought he was being too rough so they started arguing. Dad slapped him around the face and Callum's girlfriend started crying. By this point I was incredibly frustrated that I couldn't snap myself into sobriety and that my drunkenness had caused this fight. They were shouting around me while I helplessly fell about the garden and house.

Callum made up a bed on the floor for me so I would be near the bathroom during the night. He slept nearby in case I choked on my vomit. I was ill for the next few days, and delicate for the rest of the holiday. Never again have I drunk myself quite so sick.

Shortly after Gareth's overdose when he burnt his hand on the radiator, I went to visit Callum in Les Menuires, where he had been working in a hotel kitchen in the ski resort so that he could snowboard all winter. He was tanned beyond recognition and his floppy mouse brown hair had been bleached by the sun. One of my brothers was in perfect health – Callum has always known how to enjoy life. When I told him about the overdose, he thought about returning to England but I said there was nothing he could do that would make any difference and that he may as well finish the season, especially as he was due to come back in just a few weeks anyway. He and I had been planning a summer trip to Thailand for a while, but we became nervous about leaving Gareth. When Callum was back in England we asked Gareth if he wanted to come with us. Callum's logic was that if he was going to be miserable he may as well be miserable on a beautiful beach. He refused before we even had a chance to approach the hospital about it. We had an interminable debate as to whether or not we should go. It seemed as though Gareth's death was imminent. Selfishly I told Callum it was the only thing keeping me going, the thought that we'd be leaving the country. It was an endless, guilt-ridden conflict. Should we not travel in case something happened to him during the time we were away? Should we put our lives on hold?

We did go away, and before we left we took photographs of the three of us on Hampstead Heath, fooling around by one of the ponds. Gareth's hand was still bandaged, the scuffed fibres poked out from beneath the cuff of his shirt. My two brothers jumped on each other's backs and scrapped around, as they had done when they were young boys. This is how far things had gone, we thought we'd better have pictures of him in case he was dead when we got back. Photos were important to us, those documents that testified to our once having been there, together.

While we were away we called Dad whenever we could to check Gareth hadn't attempted suicide again. I was paranoid. I couldn't help thinking that he might do something straight after our last call, and that we wouldn't know until it was too late – too pointless – to return.

It was just days after Gareth's death but everything was safer once Callum was home. Late at night he and I sat in the kitchen, we ate as everyone else slept. He lavishly spread butter on water biscuits. When he was a teenager he would come home from school at lunchtime to eat a pitta bread with a sausage stuck in it. It was the only thing he would eat for lunch, then he would go back round the corner to school. At that time, after supper he would work his way through whole packets of water biscuits as he read books or newspapers for hours. Now he eats anything and everything.

We spoke of our family as though it were a black comedy. 'It makes you wonder who's next,' he said, and we laughed because there could be no other reaction. It was farcical to us, this foreboding presence of who would 'bite the bullet' next. We were exhausted. We didn't say much. I sat not really needing words from him. I was just glad he was home.

The following morning Callum left the house to go to the police station. No sooner had he left the house when he reappeared. 'The bastards have bloody clamped me.'

In the daylight a sign was perched on the wall next to his car, *NO PARKING AT ANY TIME*. In the darkness it was invisible. He called Lambeth Council to explain his circumstances, and to insist they get a street light.

'You must understand,' he was told, 'vehicle owners will say anything to get out of paying the fine. I'm very sorry about your brother but we can't make you the exception to the rules. You'll have to pay the fine before the clamp is removed.'

'But there wasn't a bloody light, I couldn't see the sign.' he persisted.

'I do apologize, but that's not my department. You'll have to follow that up once you've paid the fine.'

We needed the car so he paid the fine.

We went to the morgue to see Gareth's body with his girlfriend of a few months. She was devastated, frail because of his death. She had gone to his flat several times in the days when his body lay still, ringing the bell of a dead man's flat. He had told her he was staying with me and she hadn't known I was out of the country.

A deceitful plan to evade life.

We were advised that seeing him would be upsetting because he had decomposed quickly. I did not want to have my last vision of him annihilated, and chose not to see him. Callum wanted to because he did not believe his death to be true. I watched Gareth's bereaved girlfriend and Callum as they were guided through a narrow passageway while I waited at the end of it. They were given the impression that they were being taken somewhere through corridor after corridor, when the attendant motioned towards a glass screen they were about to walk past. She let out a scream and Callum grabbed her tight. Gareth lay behind the glass. Callum later told me that his face was green. His death mask came from bathing in the sun for too long. He was much bigger, had gained stature in death. He was unrecognizable. Callum still did not believe.

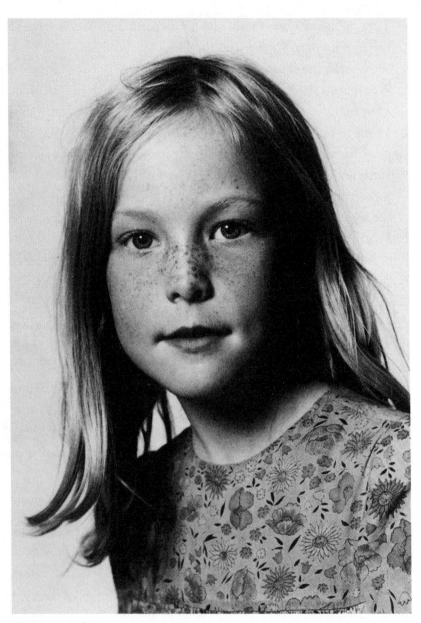

Hattie, aged 10

Chapter Three

It was different when we saw Mum. The three of us went to the hospital chapel where her body had been placed. We were asked by the kind woman who had brought us to her if we wanted to go in alone or together. Callum and Gareth said what I was thinking, alone. We must have all wanted our own chats with her. One by one we were allowed into the small room where she was. I went in first.

She lay on a table in the middle of the room, covered up to her neck in dark red velvet. I was scared to be in the room with her, scared to turn away from her. I felt she might move. The assumption of life is enduring. Her face had changed. She had died of a muscle and skin inflammatory disease, which in its later stages had attacked her face. Part of her lip seemed deformed, as if it was coming away from her face. She did not look how she once had. I don't recall what I said to her, I just remember she did not look like her. The peaceful beauty the dead are supposed to possess had been denied her. I couldn't kiss her lips, fearful that she might move, that she might have one last bit of life left in her, or that I might knock her body and cause her more indignity. I passed a kiss from my mouth to my fingers to her mouth. The most gentle of kisses. I cried. And I did not believe.

Callum and Gareth went in one after the other. They came out as vulnerable men, tears clinging to the rims of their beautiful eyes.

Callum blew his nose, loud as ever, reverberating through the room. The woman asked us if we wanted to see her again. One last chance to see your mother, ever. Both my brothers took their last chance. I didn't want to see her dead twice.

I asked the woman, 'Did she look like that when she died?' As I tried to expel the words from my mouth I began to cry, my breath quickened into the kind of hysterical crying one works up to in childhood. She explained the effects of decomposition, that she wouldn't have looked quite like that. But as we three left the hospital I remembered that there are make-up artists for the dead. Because of her illness, she would have looked worse were it not for disguising pigment.

The neck of her dead body had looked uncomfortably pulled into the material which covered her. It was drawn up to her so tightly that you couldn't help but wonder about the body underneath. It had, of course, undergone a post-mortem. The knife marks, the incisions, the sewing together of pounds of flesh. The coroner's report specified how much her brain weighed. I asked Callum how they would know that. He looked at me with kind disbelief. 'How do you think?' They had taken out her brain, her liver, her heart, her spleen, her kidneys. Her left lung weighed sixty grams more than her right. Her body was a butchered cocoon.

The report said she died from: '*1a Bronchopneumonia and 1b Dermatomyosistis*'.

It started with a transfusion to replace several pints of blood that had been lost through her menopause. After the transfusion, so swollen was her face, so black were her eyes, that her brother-in-law said she looked as though she had been beaten. The blood was needed. For months she had been functioning on rationed iron. She had carried stems of raw ginger in her bag, she would bite into them, breathing the heat on those around her, seeking warmth and energy her drained blood denied her. After weeks and months of running on empty, merely preparing a meal would banish her to bed for the rest of the day. After she'd mixed the mincemeat for the Christmas cake she made every year, she slept for days. When we were out together she would have to sit down on the street, unable to go on with the least strenuous of tasks. The line between life and death was crossed the day her limbs seized up and she could not manoeuvre her body into her bath. She lived alone and the realization that if she had got into the bath, she may not have been able to get out, led her to carry herself to hospital.

She needed a hysterectomy to stop her blood dripping away, but doctors repeatedly put the operation off because of her lack of strength. After many weeks she had the operation. A full recovery was anticipated. Doctors estimated how long she would be in hospital for. One month became two months. Two months became four months. Four months was an over-estimation. She died two months after being admitted to hospital. Her muscles became weaker and weaker. Wasted and wasted. Skin rashes that had appeared on her body after the transfusion became worse. Sores manifested themselves on her body. Her exterior was mimicking her internal self. Her organs were deprived of immune support. For a while she lost her voice, her larynx went on strike. A starving muscle, it starved her of speech. Unable to speak, when I visited her she would write down the newspapers she wanted me to buy. She could not bend her legs towards herself, so I cut her toenails. She could not steady her hand to put balm on her disintegrating lips, so I smoothed it on for her. Her body so tired of functioning it wanted to stop.

After her death a medical student friend of Callum's gave him a photocopied sheet of information about the illness:

Polymyositis-Dermatomyositis – The feature that distinguishes this disorder from other myopathies is the nature of the pathologic lesions in the muscles, i.e., degeneration of individual groups of muscle fibres accompanied by a prominent interstitial infiltrate of chronic inflammatory cells. The disease is most common in the forty- to sixty-year-old age group, but a variant affecting children between the ages of five and fifteen years is also recognized. Overall, females are affected about twice as often as males.

Typical adult dermatomyositis. This disorder is of acute or subacute onset, occurs in women, and is associated with a classic rash on the face and progressive muscular weakness.

Of interest, however, is the report of multiple cases within the same family, and the association of polymyositis with C2 deficiency and with HLA-DR 3, suggesting that genetic factors may be involved in the pathogenesis.

When my mother explained her illness in a letter to a friend twenty days before her death, it seemed as though things started to go drastically wrong after the blood transfusion. Contaminated blood perhaps.

On October 20th, I went along and had the usual routine tests including the blood test. When they'd done the blood test they called me in again. Then they started holding out chairs for me. Then they got a surgeon to say that you're supposed to have twelve something-somethings, and I only had six something-somethings which was dangerously anaemic and unheard of and I must have a blood transfusion at the weekend and a hysterectomy as soon as possible afterwards. Oh yes and also just for a bit more fun I've a massive fibroid growth in my womb which is getting bigger all the time ...

So like a good girl I go along for my transfusion feeling rather shattered by all this as I haven't felt healthier or happier for years.

As soon as the transfusion starts I don't feel right but never mind. Sunday morning I leave feeling weird. Hat comes up for half-term. My neck turns scarlet, my eyes start to itch and massive blisters start to appear behind my ears and start spreading across my scalp. Have very pleasant half-term with Hat but body is increasingly on fire. I go to the doctor who asks if I've eaten anything unusual and prescribes creams and shampoos and stuff. My body turns reddish purple.

Hat goes home and I notice when driving that it is a tremendous effort to lift my legs to change gear. A most spectacular blister appears ballooning on my side and drips all over the bed and my clothes. I go to the doctor again. Well I think the rash on your hands is going. I think we're winning. Rubbish.

One morning I wake up and notice that my face and neck and left side are amazingly puffed up. I go to the doctor and ask what on earth is happening to me. More creams and some antihistamines are prescribed.

The last three days I couldn't even bath, because I knew in the unlikely event of my succeeding in getting into the bath I would never get out.

After that with helpful naggings from my sister I had a lovely ambulance ride to the hospital on 28th November where I have been ever since.

Apparently I've got Dermatomyositis which means skin and muscle inflammation and whether or not the transfusion triggered it off that is definitely when it began. Luckily they took me in before the breathing and heart muscles went . . .

Meanwhile I am slowly, very, getting better and have the hysterectomy tomorrow. I still can't move or talk or swallow, but I won't need to will I?

For me, if anything had to go wrong, it couldn't have gone wrong at a better time. Quite blamelessly, I am totally UNABLE to do anything about the family Christmas. My guardian angel works in mysterious ways but is definitely very on the ball . . .

P.S. My romance blossoms in spite of everything, including blisters! M.

She had preferred to be ill in hospital than face the family Christmas. The year before, which was the first Christmas since she had left our home, my mother decided to come back – for our sakes. Then on Christmas Eve, Gareth – aged eighteen – took an overdose. Mum was crushed. She had tried to do the right thing and things still went wrong. I remember how torn she looked: split between anger and hopelessness at the situation. Would there ever be a time when he wouldn't pull these stunts? As always she had done everything in her power, at the expense of herself, and that wasn't enough to stop him. A part of her must have wished she'd stayed in her new home. She sat in the green chair, and exuded despair at the impossibility of reconciling devastation with acceptance.

My mother would never be able to tolerate Gareth's intent to die. But with every overdose and threat of self-damage the seriousness of his intent became clearer and clearer. Each one broke her a little more, chipped away at her as though she were some saint to be tested. The pain must have coursed through her, and yet she never screamed the scream of a mother in agony. She never picked things up and smashed them out of frustration, the way Gareth had on many occasions. She was bound to him as a mother who instinctively protects her child no matter what he does. But she didn't get the care she needed. She didn't have doctors rallying around her, as they did around Gareth, to make sure she was all right.

On the Christmas Day after the overdose we decided that we would have our lunch then take some to Gareth. We piled a bit of everything high on a plate and drove to the hospital. The streets were nearly empty. The odd car sped past us on the deserted roads. When we arrived we heated up the food in the microwave in the cafeteria, then took the steaming works up in the lift to Gareth. The ward was quiet as most of the patients had permission to leave for Christmas. Gareth was sitting up in bed. We presented him with his lunch and some presents but he didn't want to see us. He stared straight ahead, pretending we weren't there. He wouldn't look any of us in the eye and refused to eat the food we thought would make him feel cared for. All he could say to us as we stood by his bed in our unconventional family Christmas was 'Just fuck off.' His expression was one of betrayal, anger, sadness and fear. He was cross we had come to see him, but how much more so would he have been if we hadn't?

Callum was pissed off, and told Gareth so. After saying that he wasn't going to stand there and be sworn at he walked out of the ward. Then my mother, who normally silently simmered away, broke down and told him he was selfish, that he should appreciate what everyone was trying to do for him. She had come to London when she hadn't wanted to, for him and us, to give us Christmas, and this is what she got in return. It was, I think, the only time I heard her take a swipe at him. Then she and my father left together and I said I would stay a little longer. He and I had been getting along around that time and I thought he might speak to me if nobody else was around. He did, a little. He still couldn't look me in the eye, which was probably just as well because I started to cry as soon as I started to speak. I told him that we cared about him, and he replied that they didn't understand. With this 'they' he had inferred that I might. If that is what he meant, it wasn't to last.

Gareth went through phases of believing that certain people were on his side, whether it be friends, family or doctors. Then the tide would turn and they would be cast out of favour. He had faith in individual doctors while they thought they might help make him better. When it became apparent they couldn't, or when he decided they couldn't, in his mind he cut them off. Soon after talking to me that day he began to think that I was trying to destroy him. Later on he would say that Callum was the only one of our family that he could relate to. Prior to that he had claimed our mother as his protector. He knew he was paranoid, he would repeatedly tell his doctors this, but he was unable to realize that he was imposing this on us, and that really we did love him and never wanted him to perceive us as the adversaries he often did.

Because of the nature of Gareth's death there was an inquest. My father went to it. He heard the distressed policeman who had broken down Gareth's door and found his body give evidence. Dad said he'd never known a rainier day than that of the inquest – he was soaked through as he walked from King's Cross tube to the coroner's court. The cause of death was 'Amitriptylene and Coproxamol poisoning'. The former is an anti-depressant, the latter a painkiller. The local newspaper, the *Hampstead and Highgate Express*, gave his death a two by five inch space. *Man, 24, killed himself,* read the headline.

A 24 year old man 'obsessed' with taking his own life succeeded after many attempts, an inquest heard on Tuesday. Gareth Gordon, of Ainger Road, Primrose Hill, had had a difficult life, his father, a literary agent, told St Pancras coroner's court. Mr Gordon said his son had been ill all his life and his mother had died four years ago. He was found dead near bottles of pills. Dr. _____, at the Royal Free Hospital, said he had tried to kill himself five times since he was 13. Coroner Dr. _____ recorded the verdict that Mr Gordon took his own life because of his illness.

He had tried many times more than five, though he wasn't hospitalized with every attempt.

I took the tube to Kentish Town Police Station to fetch the keys to his flat. I stood in front of the reception desk and a policeman perused me. Without words he stuck his chin in the air as if to say, 'What do you want?'

'My brother killed himself. He was found on Tuesday, and you have the keys to his flat.' Still no words, he swaggered his six feet away. He came back with a small plastic bag. Inside were Gareth's keys along with the keys to the padlock the police had put on his flat's door after they forced it open, his watch, and some loose change.

Callum and I drove to his flat. We had to clear it up as soon as possible to hand it back to the housing association it belonged to. There was red tape across the door, black writing ordered, *Do Not Enter*. We ripped the tape away and unlocked the padlock. When the door opened we retched and heaved, the stench was vile and consuming. We had to breathe through our mouths to not choke on the smell of death. We rushed to the windows, threw them open for the air nestling in the tops of the trees outside. We turned back on ourselves to face his bedroom and walked towards it. We both stood in the doorway, reluctant to go in, knowing he was last alive, and dead, on that bed. Instead we walked around his flat filled with sunlight from the two long front windows. It was bewildering to know that the last person there, with the exception of the police, was him. But he would never be there again.

Callum poured oil into Gareth's wok, heated it until it was smoking, and added a concoction of the most aromatic spices. He swept through the flat holding the sizzling wok, earnestly trying to replace the rankness with a sweeter smell. While the wok was hot and cooking the spices we were given respite from the reminder of rotting flesh. When it cooled, the odour of Gareth's death lingered.

I could not be near his bedroom too much, with the knowledge of it being death's rented room, and my retching response to the smell.

Standing by the window I looked out to the street. People, guarded by their windows, looked back at me as though they knew me. They had heard and they wondered. Wanted to see, wanted to gawp. With wide eyes, they wanted to poke their noses in.

We went back to the bedroom, entered it, got close to the bed, where the smell was the worst. On blood stains, where his dying body had leaked, clans of maggots had hatched in his mattress, nourished by the aftermath of rotting flesh. It was repellent. Wriggling insects feeding on my brother's deathbed. We threw the mattress out of the front window, then debated whether to put it in a skip that was in the street, or burn it. Burning won for fear of further contamination. At the edge of the road, some distance from the parked cars, we started the fire, the cremation of his bed. A middle-aged man came out of his house, he looked shocked, pious, at the potential neighbourhood hazard. 'Do you think you should be doing that there?'

Looking up, we saw people were coming out of their houses up and down the street. They watched, but none of them said or did anything. They knew. My ever-patient brother, rather than flying into a rage, replied, 'Where would you like me to do it?'

We joked that this could have been evidence of an immaculate murder we had committed, and they were thinking it couldn't be, surely we wouldn't be burning the evidence so blatantly in front of their many greedy eyes. They didn't question it. Because they knew. They just watched.

We returned to his flat and rooted through his private possessions like searching burglars. Photographs taken during family holidays were mixed with bills, letters and diaries of his feelings kept for various doctors. Remnants of a life recorded on paper. Callum and I wanted different things. I was looking for a note he wrote a while ago, to tell me goodbye. A friend of Gareth's told me he had carried it in his wallet for some time, so that whenever and wherever he was found the note would get to me. Gareth had lost his wallet days before his death, but I, susceptible to the improbable, kept on looking. Callum was looking for photographs, memories immortal. Picturesque lies immortal.

There was a knock on the door. We anticipated having to explain away Gareth's death. Callum opened it to a teenager who chirped away. He was a stranger to us but we assumed he must have known our brother so we did not stop him as he walked his way into the flat. He babbled for a few minutes, then pointing to the bedroom he asked, 'Is this where the guy died?'

'Yes,' Callum replied.

'I'm not scared, some friends of mine are, but I'm not,' he said.

He talked the most meaningless talk, stringing together rambling chat. Wittering away, incessant verbal nonsense. He said nothing as his tongue continued to wag and his lips kept forming shapes to assist the utterance of bullshit words. So surreal was the moment that we didn't question who he was nor why he was there. Then he asked, 'Did you know the guy?'

He shut up, looked at us and backed off as his lazy brain awoke. We were the dead man's family. His bravado crumbled and fell from his cocky little face. He tried to give some explanation as to why it was a circus for him.

'Some of my family lived in the flat above.'

The family that moved out after hearing of Gareth's death because they believed the building to be cursed as a result of it. After coming face to face with the suicide's siblings he left somewhat greyer than he had looked on arrival.

That family had Gareth to thank for their gas meter reading. Repeatedly they made appointments with British Gas to have their meter read, but the matriarch refused to open the door to anyone during the day while her husband was at work. Gareth counselled scores of gasmen who arrived week after week and knocked on his door after failing to gain entrance through hers. They would apologize for being late, Gareth would explain that punctuality was not the problem. He became the mediator who informed her, through the door, that it was just the gas man with whom she herself had made the appointment. Months of failure might have dismayed another, but knowing she persistently made these appointments and therefore must need the reading, Gareth persevered, and one day, due to his negotiations, the gas man was let into the flat to read the trying numbers.

Chapter Four

I was held hostage to dreams of guilt, accusation and pain in the aftermath of Gareth's death. Stalked in the night when I should have had peace, or adventures in lands too improbable to exist. I should have been whisked away on a magic carpet, embroidery flapping in the wind as I flew towards distant magnificent oceans.

I am in our family house. Mum had it painted a pale pink, pink candy sitting comfortably in our cul-de-sac.

I hear there is somebody at the door. I answer it and there Gareth stands. He is seething, his face shines forth an explosive anger. I don't want to let him into the house, don't want to be tarnished by his state of mind, don't want to be caught in his force. A mouse in a mousetrap. As he starts opening the door that keeps only inches of safety between us, pushing what protects me, I muster all my strength in a futile attempt to keep it closed.

He has always been strong, stronger than he knew. He pours his weight into shifting the door, his liquid strength adapts to fit its awkwardness, his hand is gripping its edge, his fingernails turn a ferocious pink under the pressure. My face, which is squashed against the inside of the door, is millimetres away from his threatening flexing fingers. His breath of rage, leaping up from his chest and gushing out his mouth emits a rising mist, I feel the steam breaking my grasp. The door is opening and I am desperate.

I see Eleanor, my next-door neighbour, known as Jelly. We grew up together, she was born the year after me and as children we were inseparable. Strangers would stop us in the street and ask if we were sisters because our mannerisms and laughter were so alike. She is walking towards her house. I shout to her to help me but she doesn't see that I need her here, now, this very second. She looks up at us, at Gareth standing on the doorstep and me inside. She says hello and my heart sinks. How can she not see my dire plight? She vanishes into her house. Abruptly, he unexpectedly releases his Samson strength from the door. It is ajar and we stand facing each other as though time is standing still. I have no idea what he will do next because he is so hurt. I fear ruthlessness surfaces most when we are hurt. The pathos on his face eats into my own face, his green eyes stolen from some sea creature speak of terror and he says, 'You never loved me anyway.'

Sometimes when I woke I believed my mother and brother were still alive. They had never died. It took a moment or two before consciousness replied and re-informed me they were gone. Dreams were the only way they could walk around in my life, to and from rooms, scenarios played out as though they were true. Half of my mind wishing to convince the other half, engineers working in the dark to fool me. The two of them so genuinely remembered by my unconscious that I was grateful for its work. No matter how bad the dream, I did not care as long as they came back to me in the night.

Next I was to eat my brother. Ingest his corpse into my flesh in a butcher's trick of alchemy.

I step down wooden stairs into a vast basement. A friend and I begin preparing dinner on a monumental wooden table. We chop vegetables, copious amounts of vegetables, and toss them into a large cauldron-like pot, blackened from years of naked flames, layer upon layer of burning. We are making a stew for everyone in the house.

The mummified body of my brother, which lies on the table, is added to our stew in small sections. We didn't cut him up and there is no anatomical mess, but there he is chopped up in to pre-prepared neat pieces which we add one after the other along with diced aubergine and chunks of potato. This is normal, nothing to be afraid of. When the stew is cooked we gather around this table to sate our rumbling tummies. Only the two of us deceitful chefs know that we are all demolishing my brother, no one else is aware he passes our lips. His nutrients enter our blood stream and he becomes alive within us.

Gareth was particular about his food. When our paternal grand-mother asked him why he didn't eat boiled potatoes if he liked to eat chips, enlightening him on the fact that both were made from the same humble ingredient, Gareth replied by turning the question inside out. 'Well then, why don't you eat chips, Granny?' To this she had no answer as the last thing she, of Irish origin, was going to do was tuck into what she thought was the very downfall of the potato.

He ate a staggering amount of food. He would boil up a whole packet of spaghetti, add a jar of tomato sauce and eat it all in one sitting. He thought nothing of devouring two or three bags of chips and several sausages. Some nights he and I would go to the chip shop in South End Green near closing time with the hope that they would give him extra sausages for free – they often did.

When we went out to dinner as a family to celebrate one of our birthdays we would usually go to the Chinese restaurant on a boat on Regents Canal, a gorgeous, red wallpapered cavern with lanterns hanging from the low ceiling. As we grew up my elongated brothers had to stoop when we entered this culinary den. A feast would be placed on the table before us and we would momentarily marvel at the sight of these delicacies, then Gareth would plunge into the food as though he had been starved for days. My father said he ate like a ravenous vulture. His delicate china bowl would spill over with as much as he could strategically balance. His expertise in the art of chopsticks was unsurpassable. The chopsticks champion, he would make each mouthful a veritable mountain. Such was his pace that the rest of us hardly stood a chance of keeping up. The table became a battlefield for the survival of the fittest, or rather, the quickest.

During our early school years Mum would take us to Marine Ices on Haverstock Hill in the holidays for knickerbocker glories. They looked good. Those long glasses straight out of American diners and ice-cream parlours filled with different coloured ice creams, pink gooey sauce dripping down the sides of the softening mound filling the gaps left in the glass, fresh cream piled on top like a beehive hair-do, and finally, a sprinkling of hundreds and thousands. I admired Callum and Gareth as they ate theirs – I could only manage a bowl of vanilla ice cream with chocolate sauce.

I didn't have the desire to begin to rival my brothers' stomach capacity until my mother made sweet and sour pork. I thought I didn't like it, in the way that children tend to stick with their likes and dislikes of food, never humouring changes in taste. It was accepted that with my fussy eating I would simply go without meals now and then. But on this aberrant occasion I tried it and I liked it. I had found a dish with which I could match my brothers' capacity for consumption. I ate and ate and ate and ate, smugly, because I was on an even keel with them. Might I even manage more than they could? I put more and more away, wrapped it into my skinny little body. They were astounded I could do this, usually they finished my food off for me. Before the night was out, as a result of my impressive overeating, I threw up all of my mother's home-cooked Chinese. My brothers were pissed off I had wasted their much-loved sweet and sour pork. I never did out-eat either of them again.

There were just a few days until Gareth's funeral and I had nothing smart and black to wear for the occasion. To my mother's I wore a fitted black silk blouse and a long black skirt. A Victorian adolescent. On her Singer sewing machine she had made a full-length dark, murky-green velvet coat. She called it her opera coat. It had raised, swirling lines on it. I hated it when I was young, dismissed it as a hangover from the 1970s. I thought it would have been nice were it not for the radiating swirls. When I entered my teens I fell in love with that coat. The thought of being as tall as her in it and being able to fill it out seemed to me to be a measure of glamour and radiant womanhood. I wore it to her funeral. Callum wore his pink, blue and orange skiing jacket and his worn-out jeans. Dad disapproved but as Callum pointed out, 'Mum would want me to dress how I always dress.' He was not going to wear a suit for the funeral attendees. His logic was that you dressed for the person being buried. If he thought they'd want him to be smart, he'd put on a suit. If he knew they didn't care, why bother with tenets of respectability. Despite Gareth's unkempt appearance, he strove for a tamer look, so Callum decided to wear a suit for him.

I went out shopping for funeral attire. It was a strange feeling to be shopping for clothes that are appropriate for the dead. I knew I could wear red or some striking colour, bearing the principle that I wouldn't look like I was dressed for a funeral because I wanted to rejoice in a life, not mourn for one gone. But I had no interest in such thinking. I wanted to look like I was attending my brother's funeral, not a party for his vanishing. I tried on numerous dark clothes – they had to be dark – trousers, skirts, dresses, shirts, jumpers, all were wrong. What looks right when its purpose is to enclose you as you say goodbye to your sibling blood? A mantle for farewell. None made me ready to attend his funeral. I left empty handed, I would return the next day.

Walking around amid the crowds from shop to shop, I was priming myself for Gareth's funeral, and I was trying to act with normality when I felt the world was deranged. I was not just drifting with the meagre objective of finding clothes – I had more than one motive for the quest I had set myself. I was away from the other people who had lost him, so I did not have to face them. No face to face. I carried out this inane mission each day that was left before his funeral – it became a ritualistic preparation for his parting. As I crossed the road to go from one shop to another a builder shouted to me, 'Smile cherry, it might never happen.'

My mother's sister phoned the day before the funeral. She had changed her mind about attending it. She wanted to be there for us but said if she came it would be under false pretences. She said it wasn't so much Gareth's death that affected her as she felt she hardly knew him, but that it brought back everything about Mum and her death. How my mother didn't want Gareth to come to Oundle because she was scared if he came to her sanctuary he wouldn't leave. And because she felt Gareth was partly responsible for her death. That the weight of the anguish she felt for him had killed her. I admired her honesty.

The day of the funeral came. I went into town again, I had two hours to get the clothes. I found them quickly. A high-necked, black, knitted top, and grey trousers. Suitably dull and dark, but fitted, so I did not resemble the contents of a sack in this funereal outfit. I was still his little sister.

With my shopping bags in hand I went to the Covent Garden flower market to choose the last bit of life for him. The intense vibrant colours seemed so out of place on that day. Beauty clashed with adversity. I chose gerberas, the type clowns wear in their lapels and squirt water from. I picked out pink, orange, yellow and red ones. The brightest colours in the face of the day's designated morbidity. A clown's flower was appropriate for Gareth. Competing with his depression was the soul of an entertainer, a real Charlie Chaplin. If he wasn't devising pranks to befall others, he was a casualty of accidental cabaret himself.

One summer's day he cycled from Primrose Hill through Belsize Park, and up Hampstead High Street until he reached White Stone Pond. He intended to cycle around the pond with its bobbing boats and continue his journey to Highgate, but to his detriment he noticed a striking young lady. As he pedalled he watched the sway of her hips, her shapely legs sat on the perfect curve of high heels, the smile on her face, the rhythm of her long dark curly hair moving as she walked. So stirred was he that he didn't even notice himself pedalling his bike straight into the pond. The front wheel went in first, the rest of the bike dropped, he fell into the shallow water. When he emerged, dripping, to the raucous laughter of children, the cause of his mishap was nowhere to be seen.

Callum drove Dad and I to the funeral directors in Belsize Park. In the office we were asked to take a seat by a soft, compassionate voice. I couldn't help but wonder how those people could do that job day in and day out, and whether or not they spoke like that out of habit when they went home. Gentle lull, rolling sweetness, God forbid they bring on any upset before we reached the crematorium.

Sitting in an office before the cremation of my brother was all so inelegant – it drove me crazy. I imagined what was going to happen during the cremation. Burning through to the bones and deeper. A furnace flaming physical remains. Charring a body that only in the last few years finished growing.

The hearse with his resting body pulled up outside. It was a big coffin, as in death he had grown. It was made of beautiful wood.

Trees felled to house the dead. Callum and I had had a whole discussion about which coffin to get. We didn't want an extravagant coffin for him, after all it was going to be burnt, and we didn't like them anyway. Gareth wasn't a frills around the edges person, he liked minimalism.

The grand black car glided up Hampstead High Street, winding slowly like an anaesthetized snake. We followed in Callum's car. On the street, outside the inching car, people were milling about, shopping, eating and drinking in restaurants and cafes. Their movement was out of time with ours. They were still in rhythm with life, cavorting with the everyday. In that car, encased by aluminium, following another car, being followed by other cars, we were in slow motion. Like a videotape stuck on freeze frame with no button to release the trance. In death are we to become still?

I wondered if latecomers to his funeral were zooming across London, taking on red lights, getting caught by speed cameras. Stuck in traffic and swearing their heads off, anticipating the late entrance they didn't want to make, letting tempers roll before they walked in to the crematorium, heads bowed in a neat blend of embarrassment and respect. He would have laughed if they were – humour was prized by Gareth.

We arrived at the West Chapel of Golders Green crematorium. Few family members were there, but many friends of Gareth and hospital staff were gathered. Flowers were laid out across the terrace, arranged at the frozen feet of the many cement pillars. Big bunches, small bunches, roses given with tenderness, giving love that couldn't be responded to. Attached to them were cards from people who wanted to say goodbye. Messages to the dead. 'I hope you're happy now.' 'You must have found peace at last.' Hope and assumption of happiness prevailed.

Inside the chapel my father was standing on my left and Callum on my right, the three of us in the front pew. Front row seats to see the show. I hated being there because everyone behind us could see how we were. I thought I might howl the walls down. If we were in a great church would it have collapsed under the weight of his sin? Protestant brick after brick would tumble down inwards, wreck us all, leave us powdered grey with dust and debris. Grey like the cement pillars outside. His new wooden home would be deserted in the centre of a virtuous Latin cross. Windows would crash, coloured glass tinkling on the rubble, stained crystals piling up. Desecration in thought.

I didn't know if a god was there as my brother's body and life and death were solemnly celebrated prior to being flamed by oranges and blues. But it was raining. Rain that seemed as though it might empty the sky of its water, just as Gareth had wished. Rain that beat and swept the hard ground. Rogue rain, it danced, cheated as it ran across the hardened tar.

He had chosen his own requiem. For years before his death he had said he wanted to be buried in the rain to a Jean Michel Jarre track. That music was comical to me, we needed no melodramatic soundtrack. Having his body boxed in front of us was raw enough. There it sat on a raised platform, the object of the audience. But it was one of the few things he wanted that we could give.

The Minister of Ceremonies, the Reverend, made no mention of the manner of his death. Suicide would not be broached. No inference of that conundrum which defies religious teachings. No questioning as to how a person could be so dead inside that they wanted to end it all for good.

Gareth had questioned established beliefs. When Jehovah's Witnesses came to our house on their perennial rounds of door-to-door attempts at initiation, they momentarily thought they'd caught a potential convert. Gareth was only too happy to talk, he wanted an answer. He ran rings around their learned fluency with awkward questioning. He demanded to know why he was so miserable. Eventually they would retreat, unable to withstand the unanswerable questions of this stubborn man who would not be fobbed off. I think he wanted to believe, but couldn't without an explanation for his state of mind. Gareth didn't want a salesman guru, he wanted to make sense of what felt like an undeserved penance.

I cried at my brother's funeral in a way I hadn't at my mother's. I could no longer hold it in. It was not a choice as it had been when she died, to appear strong and self-contained.

Torrents of empty aching throttled me. His endured suffering was the worst, worse than his dying. It was hard for my father to see me cry. I might have been a catalyst if I'd carried on, my grief contagious. Callum put his arm around me. I knew I was making it worse for them. The pain of seeing a loved one hurt when one is hurting about the same thing is a confined and effective torture. But I couldn't stop. I wanted to scream, let hysteria loose. So I didn't stay silent but nor did I bawl and holler.

Gareth had composed a piece of music several months before he died which we played in the crematorium. Sufficiently eccentric for Gareth, he called it 'Raining on a Blue Mouse'. It was dramatic in some places, a drifting lullaby in others. As it played his spirit fluttered through the congregation of people, darting between gaps like the trails of light left by cars filmed at night. The stains of neon hung heavy. His coffin disappeared, drawn back on an electrically motivated platform. He was taken away again. We walked out of the crematorium first, Dad, Callum and myself. The others followed.

After the service we drove to the Roebuck pub on Pond Street, opposite the Royal Free Hospital. We decided to go there because it was his local in as much as he had one, and his friends all knew the place as well.

Both warmth and dire isolation hung in the air. People gather to celebrate one person's life most sincerely when they are dead. The fondness for Gareth, who had been so difficult in life, was mighty and undiminished in those that came to see him off. Callum stood up and declared, 'The drinks are on Gareth!' We had found 250 pounds in his flat when we cleared it up and we put it behind the bar. We suspected that getting drunk was as good a response to the occasion as any.

In the pub we laughed hard, remembering his humour without a trace of bitterness. Friends from our childhood and young adulthood gathered. We sat close, huddled in groups over sticky tables and remembered Gareth's spirit instead of his downtrodden heart. Clearly, he was loved. Whether any love could have been enough to sidetrack his death wish was a remote possibility. We relived the funny moments.

The time when he was a tipsy sixteen-year-old after a Christmas party, and for some unknown reason decided to get under a jeep that was parked in our street. We couldn't remember if he'd edged under there to look at the workings of such a machine, or if he was hiding, or if he was so drunk he wanted to sleep in the place that was nearest to him, outside but protected, which happened to be the road beneath the jeep.

When he went around his hospital ward with a tape recorder and a microphone interviewing patients and recorded a kind of documentary radio show on the sexual antics of his fellow patients, specifying who had slept with who, where, and when.

How he'd charmed his girlfriend on demand by opening his eyes ever so gradually so that his enviable upper and lower eyelashes separated from each other as if he were an animal emerging from hibernation, covering and uncovering his eyes – eyes whose colour came from nobody in our family. His green stood out against the rest of our blues. He was enchanting and gentle when refraining from damage.

As adolescents he and Callum put smoke bombs outside people's houses then knocked on their door so they would be warned of what appeared to be the imminent burning down of their house. They did this to a mother and daughter who lived on the other side of the road from us. The daughter came running to the door in her nightdress with her favourite teddy bears, rescuing what she could in such a short time. Her mother came screaming with saucepans of water to put the fire out. Meanwhile my brothers hid behind the bushes of the pranked duo's garden, hands held firmly over mouths to keep from hyperventilating with laughter.

Callum and Gareth fooled around in our garden and took photographs of themselves in profile pissing a huge jet of water. The jet rose up nearly as high as them, which was of course from the garden hose discreetly held down next to their trouser crotch.

Gareth loved to taunt me with my childish phobias. On one of our family narrow boat holidays he and I shared a bunk bed. I slept above and he below. He had a habit of falling out of whatever bed he slept in, often waking to find himself on the floor, so for safety's sake he always took the bed closest to the ground. As I was getting into bed one night, I opened my sleeping bag to be greeted with a flying mass of daddy long-legs which he had laboriously collected and stuffed inside. He had gone to the trouble of gathering those poor creatures just to get a scream out of me, he got what he wanted and staggered around the boat laughing like an idiot.

After he and I saw Francis Ford Coppola's *Dracula*, hungry, we went shopping for fruit in a local supermarket. Gareth turned his back to me and stuck the ends of two bananas in his mouth to mimic and exaggerate Dracula's fangs, then turned to me with a primitive husky growl. The man working the till kept an absolutely straight face and asked Gareth if he could take the bananas out of his mouth for a minute so that he could weigh them.

When we were children we went on a day trip to Calais. Gareth was especially excited because he'd heard that you could get really amazing bangers there. Sure enough, practically as soon as we drove off the boat and got out of the car we came across a man in the street selling the playful explosives. He was sturdy, particularly around his waist. He had that kind of belly that isn't fat, it has merely expanded to be a rotund form in its own right. He had a thick white beard and was perched on a stool which looked precarious under his weight. In front of him all his bangers were laid out, like the loot of long-lost treasure. Gareth asked if he had more, bigger ones. He didn't speak French and the man didn't speak English, so Gareth held his hands up with his palms facing each other and indicated how big he wanted them to be. The man brought some out from under the table from a secret stock clearly reserved for the banger dedicatee, Gareth kept widening the parameters with each new offering. As he seemed to be able to deliver the goods for each request, Gareth's requests became more fantastically demanding. They settled on a substantial collection with a ton of little ones thrown in for good measure. By then Gareth had a grin, the mischievous one that hadn't left him since he was a child. As we walked through the streets of Calais he threw the bangers here and there with great satisfaction, shocking birds into fleeing from the noise.

Reeking of a tale that could only come from Gareth's life, was the time when I had to get the morning after pill for his girlfriend. One day when I went to see him in hospital he was livid. He had been under the impression that his girlfriend was on the pill. He discovered, after the event, she wasn't. She didn't want to take the morning after pill and he didn't want to become a father. No doubt in part because a child would have made it harder for him to leave the world. He had been reluctant to get involved at all because he didn't want her grieving for him down the line, let alone face the prospect of children. And I despaired at the thought of him becoming a father when he wasn't capable of looking after himself. He seemed to think that if someone else were to get the prescription his girlfriend might take it. It was the Christmas holiday and my doctor's surgery was closed, so to get the prescription I had to see someone at the Royal Free. I went and saw a doctor a few floors above Gareth, and answered all the relevant questions. How long was it since I'd had sexual intercourse? When was my last period? Are my periods regular? What form of contraception do I normally use? The good doctor gave me the pills and I took the lift down to Gareth's ward. I handed them over and he was, I think, the most relieved I had ever seen him.

It was precious bringing back to life the tall, hilarious, sad, depressed man. We refused to admit all was lost, because it wasn't. He had been there and then he was gone, but never would he be whitewashed from our memories.

When the money in the pub ran out many people went home. We were warmly drunk with loose limbs and loose emotions but there was no rampage of histrionics. Those of us remaining moved on to an Italian cafe up the street, round the corner and down the high street. We ate bread to soak up the alcohol and chocolate cake and tiramisu laced with rum. It was dark, the lights of other cafes spotted the street. We sat outside, snug in that mild September. Summer was coming to an end and some of the trees were scantily clad. Orange and yellow leaves crunched under our feet. The moon was perfect, it looked like a biscuit, so unreal that someone might have placed it up in the sky to fool us.

There was more talk of his larking. We who knew him, had known him, long ago conceded to his clowning partnering his depression. We embraced his spicy, dry and devious sense of humour. There was an affection and acceptance over his death that evening. We just wanted to remember him, not mourn because he was gone. But I didn't know if it could remain, that state of believing his death was permissible because he'd asked for it. We stayed there for as long as we could, ordering more cake and more red wine, making the recognition of him last. We savoured his memory, soaked up every ounce, lapped it up. The last supper. Reluctant to finalize his day.

If a stranger, a passer-by, had looked at us, they never would have known we were saying goodbye.

A couple of weeks later I left my father's house and returned to university for the start of a new academic year. Before his funeral I thought life after it would get back to normal, whatever that might mean. Instead, I started to lose my mind.

Giles and Margaret

Chapter Five

I know the sister who resides in pain. She who lost when you won your death. The sister that got trapped as she was when you passed away. Always a child to an older brother. The sister caught near your death. The sister that aged. Felt worn away at twenty-one.

At first I pretend I'm fine. Then it becomes apparent I'm not. I want to live all the more because they are both dead. I try. But I can't.

Grief deadens the living. A slow pungent numbness seeks out your marrow, chafing your innermost gut. Different to the extremes of emotion, to brief highs and the depths of despair. A state of paralysis ensues. Survival requires a certain dazing of the intellect and emotions. Knowing and feeling might scar too much. In this state, withholding the mind and body a footing, you drop, lowered by willing ropes to minefields where the actions of the deceased don't seem so stupid after all.

I cross roads in blinding sunlight and am not too bothered about the outcome. The sparkling whiteness shields my eyes from the speed coming my way. I see things differently. Once harmless shapes that make up this world become instruments of threat. Class A cooking knives are for slicing veins, as are shiny razors. Any brand will do. Tall buildings are generous hosts for jumpers. Belts and ropes are for hanging. Aspirins aren't for headaches, but to nullify the bodies that belong to aching lives. Suggested dosage, forty to fifty to kill the pain.

Glistening eyes and bared, sharp teeth tempt me to come, to follow then to wonderland. They call with songs that justify the irrational. I lie on my bed and witness my imaginary fall from the window next to it, and I feel the freedom death must hold. My soul slipping free from my body. My head getting lighter, lighter. My eyes peer out to the possibility of death. Death is so close to me I am forced to befriend it, hand in hand, the sweet danger of embracing it. A careless flirtation, so close, so intimate, so easy. It could well be engulfing.

The assumption that we'll fight hard to keep life alive is, perhaps, inaccurate. I long to see those two faces, those faces that have now, no doubt, mutated in my mind. If I could die, just momentarily, so that I could see you both. Sometimes the ease of death and the sting of life feels too persuasive. I envy you both, while knowing I cannot leave. Sometimes I feel I tread the line between our two worlds, that the two collide in mine.

They keep coming into my life, wandering into my thoughts as if they have every right. Ghosts that force me to recollect, even sometimes against my will. Leave me to forget about you or else you'll drive me mad because I want you back.

Of the two of them, Gareth is the worst. I feel his presence, fleeting, like tasting liquor on someone's lips when you kiss them goodbye after a drink. Wanting to imagine they are still around in body when they are dead. Rationale versus blind yearning. Yearning desires an appearance. Just one more. One last curtain call. The finality of it is the unbearable bit. Memories ought to be enough. Growing up with someone, you store an awful lot of memories. Moments can be conjured from the mind as if it were a library. Bring them out, use them as assurance that those times existed, like the re-reading of a favourite book. The story happened. It doesn't work. Pretend it does, but it doesn't. I am steeped in the privilege of having had the real thing. I envisage his walk, the loping gait, the tall man next to me who is, was, my brother. Imaginings designed to bring him back. Come back. Just for an instant. Just to tell us if you're fine. Come back to walk again by my side. Once more. Please. How unfair of me to ask when I know you wanted to be gone. I dread that the mind will forget, that our times together will lapse into indistinction. Let you go because it's full of other stuff. Can't juggle to keep it all in there, if there's no room left in the storehouse, it might let you go.

Brothers don't die, I tell myself, and I want this to be true. They grow up, are always going to be older than you if they were born before you. How could I outlive him? Always, they are bigger than their little sister. Hopefully wiser too. They don't get put away in wards with others estranged from rationality. They don't lead their lives away from home. They don't get found on rooftops beckoning a cloud of air to take them down to the dirty ground – a ground with fag ends, spilt coke and beer, butts of cinema tickets dropped outside the theatre. They don't want to leave us because they're one of us.

But they might escape. Suicide is the great escape. The best running away you could ever accomplish.

I search old photo albums for clues, for some semblance of connection. To order pages of a mixed-up script. Hunting for our family, a visual testament that we were people in a family, that it is not a fantasy that we were once alive, together. I crave proof that I am tied to these streams of blood which now serve to confuse me. There are hundreds of pictures of us when we were little, a friend of the family is a photographer. Images of us in everyday baby and toddler action are plentiful. Gareth stands in his green flares with a goldfish patch on his knee. Both he and Callum look like they may be toppled over by their overgrown 1970s haircuts. They sit on the gate outside our house, one was blonde, the other chocolate brown. Urchins contemplating their next caper. They pass me between them, looking at baby me as though I'm some rare specimen to be studied. In one set of pictures Gareth and I are on the sitting room floor in front of the navy blue sofa. I lie on my front like a seal waiting to manoeuvre forwards and he, also lying on his front just a few inches away from my seal self, looks at me with a smiling curiosity. His eyes crinkle in this smile. He was gentle towards me before we started fighting.

My mother rarely smiled in pictures. The pictures of her smiling can be counted on one hand.

I remember the screaming ringing out in the night. I must have been eight or nine. I sat hunched up in bed, crying, trying to be quiet so that I would not be heard to be upset. Gareth had locked himself into the tiny toilet on the landing between his and our parents' bedroom. He could barely breathe for sobbing. God knows what self-harm he was doing in there, I could hear pounding against the door. My father stood outside it asking him to come out, my mother was also trying to coax Gareth out. She cried too. Callum was silent to the point that I didn't know if he was there. He always seemed to disappear in those moments of wanting to look away.

I was so used to keeping quiet that when someone tried to break into the house in the middle of the night, and through the dark I could just see the hand that thrust down the handle of the back door, trying to open it, I remained silent. I lay back in my bed, knowing to keep dumb. I ran through the whole event. He'd get into the house, he'd think people were sleeping, hopefully he'd take whatever he wanted and then leave.

After some time Gareth's cries drifted into stillness.

The next morning I awoke having wet myself. Regularly I would wake up in a warm wet patch, and have to peel my pyjamas away from the terry-towelling sheet as I got up, damp and smelling of urine. My mother never made a fuss or said anything about it. She just took the sodden sheets off the sagging mattress and made up a clean bed for me. She didn't remove the plastic sheet that covered the mattress for years. I was the one who got rid of it when I started changing the sheets on my bed. Once a year, when we were weighed and measured in the most basic of health checks, the school nurse whom I had befriended, a warm woman, looked into my file and asked if the bed-wetting had stopped yet. She enquired about my family, 'Is everything fine at home?' I didn't know what she wanted me to say so I didn't say anything.

Gareth screamed again in the night. Like chairs scraping on tiled floors, like nails running lines down a blackboard, like a fork that misses the last morsel of food and gives the plate a screeching voice. Desperation in his rasping breaths. He was throwing things from his bedroom window, from the very top of the house. They fell past my bedroom window. The soda stream machine my mother couldn't afford to buy but bought anyway to give Gareth a piece of short-lived entertainment, flew past like a plastic missile. Mugs, gathered in his room from numerous cups of tea, crashed to the ground. China broke on paving stones. I could hear my mother trying to hold him back. I wondered if the objects were in place of himself. A drop of four floors. In the morning the shattered pieces were distributed over the back of the garden, a messy mosaic. Mum looked the same as she often did, forlorn and in need of leaving. I don't think Gareth rose from his bed that day. Weeks later I found the soda stream pipe and lever in the garden. Chips of china found their way into my hands. None of them matched as many cups had been broken.

Years later, when our mother was dead and Gareth and I had befriended each other, he suggested that it would be funny to throw a mass of china from his window. He threw a couple of mugs crashing down and laughed so incredibly hard that I thought he might rupture his insides. With a wincing ache I thought of Mum and I picking up the broken pieces of soda stream and china from the last time he'd piled up the crockery.

I wish he would appear before me when I'm half asleep to tell me what he is up to. I worry that he will be reborn into the same life, or that orthodox Christians were right he will be eternally damned.

I think of the Harpies in Dante's Hell, attacking those who have been turned into trees because they chose to leave. Tearing at their leaves while they scream. Eternally bound to that existence, only bleeding and mourning as time passes. Being sentenced to eternity because they were miserable.

Gareth had spoken of dying as a way to get freedom. I don't remember him ever fearing what might happen afterwards. If he would disappear, if his soul would vanish into an underworld, if his spirit would lag on, keep going despite his wishes. Maybe he thought it would all be better. That's what I think, have to think. It is too hard to contemplate him still being in pain after all his efforts to stop it. What if the end is not the end? That would have terrified him had he entertained the possibility.

I hear the screaming of those trees. Voices of damnation left to be tortured by their actions. They were condemned for rejecting the body. In my dreams I fight the gods to free him, to let him go if I promise to stay. Make deals with the powers that be so that he may not be kept. My imagination takes things and runs with them, sees him trapped by the hospital tubes sticking into him that were supposed to save him.

I write to a Tibetan Buddhist nun I'd met before he died and asked what will happen to him according to Buddhist belief. Will he be recycled, or will he begin again where he left off? I don't receive a reply and I blame Indian post rather than a reluctance on her part to tell me what she knew I would not have wanted to hear. I don't bond with any scriptural explanation, like a child I make up my own. He has gone somewhere where he will be deeply protected and made to feel better and he will come back, but not to the same, torn, tensile horror. And I am pious in my belief that any way other than death would have been unlikely for him. It is my line of defence, all I can do to persuade myself to accept.

I go to the counselling office at my university. I explain what has happened, that I was seeing a counsellor before the summer and that we mutually decided to end our sessions, but as my brother committed suicide four weeks ago I would like to start seeing her again. The receptionist asks for the name of my counsellor and then makes me an appointment with her.

Several days later I arrive for my session and go into the room I am directed to, where a stranger joins me.

'Oh, you must have wanted to see the other Susan.'

I am baffled. If there are two counsellors with the same name why didn't the receptionist ask me which one I wanted, or why did she not look up who had been treating me? The woman before me says she can deal with me for this session if I wish. As I'm already there I take up her offer. She asks me what has happened, I begin the tale of events. The straight facts come out of my mouth, as simple as if I'm describing a scene from a film. This happened then that happened, then this happened then that happened. Despite the pained look upon her face I bear no guilt as the one who listens wrestles with my outpour. It is her job to listen. What did she expect?

'Well I think it's best if you see Susan, seeing as she knows the history to all this. There really isn't much point in us getting into it is there,' she says, after twenty minutes, whilst I am in mid-flow.

This is not a question for me to answer. She has answered it herself. I walk away.

The receptionist asks if I wish to make another appointment.

'No, thank you.' I will not be burned twice.

Being so calm, whilst embedded in a state of shock, you drift, strangely aware of what's going on around you. But none of it is real. Going through the day as if in a trance. Life becomes unreal when death deals a personal blow. It is like a drug which doesn't suit, which doesn't sit well in the body. It reacts against it, doesn't allay hurt but breeds it. The waiting game. Death teaches patience like nothing else because there is no choice. Time will heal they say. Time earns you the right to live with things, but insides buckle when a reminder strikes a chord.

I am functioning. I go through situations I went through before he died without a second thought, feeling like an alien. The slightest thing is draining. Going to the supermarket I might see a man who has some similar characteristic to Gareth. A slope of a shoulder, a slouch, or the same shaggy haircut that was the result of blindly taking scissors to his own hair. Such chance occurrences unnerve me but I like them. It is a glimpse of something no longer here, enabling me to persuade myself he still roams supermarkets looking for banana fangs.

I start to see Mum too. There is a reflection of her in the television when it's not on, shadow on grey, a silhouette of her. I am reluctant to move because the shape could change. If I stay still long enough she appears for me like a shadow puppet. It is the outline of her face, I know it is. She is hanging around so that I may see her. She is telling me it doesn't matter that she is gone because she can come back to us. When I move the dust takes over and wipes away her place. Their souls may have existed still, but their bodies are invisible, cremated, turned to dust.

I yearn to be little again so that I can remember what it was like to be close to her. To have her hold and protect me as she did when I was a child. This time, I promise, I will remember.

Going out at night with friends seems absurd. I should have stayed at home, retreated as soon as he died, mourned as people used to mourn in days old. But to cut the tenuous threads of living might be too dangerous, if you do you mightn't come back. I stand by the bar, my friends drink and dance around me, they behave as most of them are, young and free. Playing with no menace in their thoughts.

What was his last thought before he died? Did his liver blow up before or after he was unconscious? Did he really start to decompose that quickly? Can I not fool myself enough to think he was in a lengthy deep sleep, not rotting immediately after his blood stopped coursing through his arteries?

My friends show me how to stay alive. They know that my blood pumps even though his world ended. They encourage me to leave the house, accompany me into town, ask nothing too strenuous of me. One puts flowers in my bedroom with a card that reads, 'This is just a reminder of the impermanence of beauty.' Such precious gestures from my friends that Gareth will never know. They leave cups of tea outside my bedroom when I refuse to come out because I cannot face myself let alone another person. They care for me but they don't patronize – and they don't stop. And they are too young to look after a grieving sister so I appreciate their tenderness even more.

I am guilty. I want him back yet I experience relief now that he is gone. Though with this relief is an absence. Something is missing and it isn't just Gareth, it is a way of life that is founded upon waiting. Waiting for the call, the ending. It hits me each morning. Never again will there be a phone call to say he's in hospital. It is foreign to my legs and arms and hands and head not to have Gareth to visit in hospital. I am divested of what was, for so long, his potentially imminent death. The ending has happened, so where do we go from here?

I am starting to become afraid of the dark, slowly. Alone in the dark is when fear creeps into my bones. Oozing, like seeping black lava. Alone in the dark, silence has a monopoly that refuses to keep at bay what has happened. Nocturnal calmness is corrupted and sleep at night has become an aberration. And the waking hours are like someone else's dream. I get out of bed at four in the morning and make toast. The kitchen light is reflected in the night's windows. As the smell of the browning bread fills the house and the friends I live with sleep, things seem as though they might get back to normal. Granary bread with masses of butter. Hungry for sustenance. I lean against the cupboards, the sound of my teeth biting into the toast is loud, it breaks the quiet.

His death has made me scared of time. Of time's right to slip away like sand held tightly in the palm of a hand. It is evasive, allusive, doggedly persistent in its betrayal. It walks ahead of you, not with you. We are always, at the very least, one step behind time. And when a loved one is now late to meet me, or worse, does not turn up at all, I see car crashes. I map out the possible endings. They would have made it had they not skidded on the threadbare tyres that should have been changed. If they had turned a moment earlier or later, if they had turned the corner when the other car wasn't coming. Or if some drunk hadn't got into their car. 'I can handle my drink.' So why the crash? Or they were walking past a building in London when a bomb went off. Their flesh exploded before they were due to meet me. I get ready for the officer who's going to tell me the news. Of course he or she won't know about the others, that another of their colleagues had stood in front of me as they do now. Savage disappearance. Don't attach because they'll go, say the voices, demented voices, but speaking only of what they know. I imagine this with one foot in one world, that of the dead, and one foot in another, that of life. In limbo, which will come to dominate the day isn't known. It's just a guess until there is a phone call or an appearance. And then they appear and I am the fool.

As it turns out, everyone has a story of suicide. It was either a friend or a friend of a friend or a family member or a long-lost relative or a lover. This act which is to many a taboo, that makes people's jaws drop when you tell them, that they find hard to believe, is so common. Few are innocent of the experience. I wonder why shock is the prevalent reaction I receive when I reveal that my brother has done himself in. And when people ask how many brothers and sisters I have I tell them about Callum, and then I have to tell them about Gareth, as to deny his existence by not mentioning him seems like a betrayal, some faces wear horror then, too. But I can't hide him. Silence is too dangerous – things rot, fester and mutate. If they can't handle my words, if they find them thorny, thick-skinned or callous, tough.

When my mother died there was no stigma. There was devastation. There were phone calls in which people asked to speak to her and I had to tell them they couldn't because she was dead. There were obituaries in the national newspapers. There were countless streams of tears. But there was no stigma.

Now that Gareth is dead, some eyes scowl after I've revealed the fact. How unreal and how disgusting and how appalling and how impossible to live with. The looks on people's faces when they know. Like I'd slept with my best friend's lover or killed a newborn baby. Shock on faces is so readable. The astonishment that follows the spillage, the widening eyes that form a fixed gaze, as though staring were restorative and might re-consume the words enunciated.

The law used to say you couldn't die by your own hand. Today suicide isn't illegal, it is a stain on a person's history. It is an insurmountable *faux pas*, destined never to sit comfortably with cancer or good old-fashioned heart failure. It raises too many questions. They want to ask why, but know the answer might contain a whole barrage of facts that make them regret they had ever asked.

I am in the queue at my university café. I want a cup of tea. The friend I'm with asks how things unfolded exactly, she wants to know the sequence of events. I relay what happened, I end by telling her the police found Gareth's body. The tea lady butts in.

'He's lucky he was found.'

I ignore her. It's just a daft remark. It's not her fault. With my lips together I give her a pursed half smile. I just want my tea. She keeps going.

'No I mean it. You hear some stories today.'

Still it is not her fault, her optimism assumes too much. But she continues.

'He's lucky to be alive.'

'He's not.'

Her eyes have just seen the plague. She has impaled herself on her hope. Still it is not her fault.

'Oh, I'm sorry, it's just that I thought . . .'

These confrontations pursue me, follow me like I am an idiot magnet.

When I see older, depressed people, people on the streets completely lost, I know Gareth could have become that, and it seems safer that he is gone. I wonder what it would be like if he were not dead, if he were alive. Though I don't see this. Never can I believe in his endurance. Gareth believed that we are living in a hell on earth, that things were so lousy it must be hell.

Once he asked me how I would feel if he were to succeed in his gamble of Russian roulette. I replied that I would be devastated but would understand. I didn't know whether he would be able to live a long life when I said this. Brought up by my mother in the art of walking on eggshells, I chose not to aggravate his guilt. Maybe it was a ridiculous thing to say, I practically handed him my consent for his ambition to die.

I have read books on suicide that tell you how to discern if a person wants to kill their self, how to pick up clues from his or her language and behaviour. But the books don't tell you what to do if that person has openly told you and everyone else they know that they plan to do it, and have been committed, but are insistent they will eventually carry out the act.

His death had been a possibility for such a long time it seemed as though it might be a realistic outcome. And if it were, I thought, understanding would naturally follow.

I am on the bus with a friend. She too wants to know what happened. I tell her. The police broke the lock to get into his flat and found his body. The story doesn't change. She is asking many questions, she wants all the facts to know what I have been through so that she can help me. We rise from our seats to get off the bus, the woman sitting behind starts shouting at us.

'You young people today are disgusting. The filth that comes out of your mouth is vile. You are so screwed up.'

Taken aback, we don't believe this is happening. This woman wants to designate the quarters where I can speak about my brother. She listened to every word and then told us how screwed up we were. She chose to take it in, consume what disgusted her so that she could vilify us. The truth is ugly for her. Would she rather hear sweet talk, niceties as she rides the bus?

It may be unpalatable to hear, but it is shameful to run and hide, crouching from truths. To do so makes you destitute in your own past. The things you wish never happened. Wipe away what offends your ears and turn it into taboo. Best we should never hear it.

93

Margaret with Callum, 1969

Chapter Six

In my grief over Gareth, I have started to mourn my mother.

I was a stunned fifteen-year-old when she died, now her death tracks me down with virulent beatings on the walls of my stomach. My resistance starts to burn, fiercely, because I waited. Residing under my skin is an anger barely harboured by its armour. It seethes under the surface, ready to break free at any moment.

For years I have believed it was all right that she died because it meant she had at last found peace and rest. She didn't have to look after Gareth any more, her youngest son. Not search for a cure to ensure his survival, not admit he wanted to die; his gestating will to abandon corporeal ownership. She no longer waits for the next overdose, the next trip to the hospital, the next unconscious scene in intensive care. For life-saving tubes to be inserted into his body. When my mother died she was tired and worn out. At the time, I thought her death a life improvement. Can't pretend any more though. It is not all right at all. She is gone.

I found out she had died from her brother, Uncle John.

Jelly had spent the night at our house. That night, we had talked until it was late and she decided to stay and share my bed. The phone had been ringing incessantly so I took it off the hook before we went to sleep. We were woken up on the morning of New Year's Eve at about nine by the doorbell. In my nightdress I ran down the two flights of stairs from my bedroom and swung open the front door, worried I'd miss whoever it was. An incredibly long, blond policeman peered down at me and took out his little notebook.

'Hello, sorry to disturb you, are you ...' He searched for my name in his notebook, '... Harriet Gordon?'

'Yes. Why?' I replied, bemused. I hadn't done anything for which I could be expecting a visit from the police.

'We've had a call from ...' He looked down again as his eyebrows performed all kinds of acrobatics. '...an Uncle John of yours. He's been trying to get hold of you since the early hours of the morning. He says he hasn't been able to get through to you on the phone.'

'Do you know why he's been calling?'

'No, I'm afraid I don't.'

I told him I would call my uncle, and he left down the ten or twelve steps that led people up to and away from our front door. His heavy black shoes guided his gangly legs, as if they needed to be weighed down.

I knew it was important. I rarely saw my uncle and much less spoke to him on the phone. It must have been urgent for him to have called the police. I became anxious. What could it be? Jelly said she'd leave while I spoke to him, she knew I didn't like dealing with serious things in front of other people. I phoned him, asked him how he was and he said nothing else before saying,

'Harriet, I'm afraid I have some very bad news.' I had no idea what was coming next. I kept quiet. 'Your mother died this morning.'

I don't remember what I said back to him. I got off the phone as soon as I could, seconds after the words had been let loose. I was unable to speak. I walked up and down the stairs in the darkened hallways, dark because I hadn't yet opened the curtains, unable to see through my tears, not knowing where to go. I had to move. I couldn't stand still. I didn't go to the bottom of the house because Gareth was asleep down there and I was scared of how he would react to what I would have to tell him. I pressed my hands tightly over my mouth so that he wouldn't hear my cries.

My mother had collected old mirrors. She discovered them, then hung them on our walls. They were all over the house, she had left them in situ when she moved out less than two years earlier. Two in the living room, one in the bathroom, one above the stairs leading to what had once been her and my father's bedroom, and one on the stairs leading from the bathroom down to the living room. Strangely, given this weakness, she was not vain. She couldn't be bothered, nor did she have the time to be. She liked the muted golden gilt of their frames, the shine mottled with time, just as she often preferred frames around works of art to the artwork in them, and maybe she liked the reflection. The fall of light on objects demanding to be known. Mirrors leave no corner left unturned. They catch in their edges the things you wouldn't normally notice. The one above the stairs pinched our feet as we descended, step by step our legs came into view. Our bodies were dismembered every time we raced down that staircase. The one on the next staircase down caught the door of the sitting room and anyone who entered or exited the room. Maybe to her, an artist, mirrors were primed fleeting canvases. They snap many scenes in a day, detect anyone who scampers past, or one who leisurely checks their appearance. Those mirrors lived with a permanent picture of carpeted stairs, or wooden banisters painted white, but were treated to varied daily comings and goings.

They followed me, devised my entrapment and forced me to see myself there. I couldn't seem to get out. It was as though the whole house was turned into a mirror to taunt me because I didn't want to be in it at that moment. I couldn't go down a flight of stairs without catching a glimpse of me in a frame. In my reflection I saw myself crying for my mother, feeling what I didn't want to feel. Hostile mirrors reflect hostile times. Leave me alone, get out of my face. Don't want to see myself here. I sat on the stairs trying to be silent when what I wanted to do was scream.

I called my father who was in Glasgow with his girlfriend. I told him Mum was dead. He said he would come back and I told him not to, to which he inevitably said, 'Of course I'm coming back.'

'Well don't come back for me because I'll be fine,' I said, desperately wanting to sound as though I were. He wouldn't be able to do anything, wouldn't be able to change anything – no one could – so I didn't want to see him.

I called Jelly and told her the impossible news. I didn't know what to do. I didn't know who or what I wanted. I wanted someone but they were all wrong. She came over to the house, she was crying and I realized I couldn't see anyone because they would steal the tears I felt I was not allowed to cry.

My school friend Sami called, as she did everyday, and I told her what had happened. She said I shouldn't be on my own, I stressed that I didn't want to see anyone and asked her not to come to the house.

I hid in my bedroom with the door tightly shut. I found the pictures my mother and I had taken in a passport photo booth just a few months earlier. We had both pulled stupid faces, I stuck my tongue out, so did she. We widened our eyes in a daft, exaggerated expression. Her face was strained though, even when acting like a five-year-old. I found the doll she bought for me not long ago in a flea market she and I went to near where she lived. Lived. Tilly the rag-doll. I didn't have dolls when I was a child, I had fluffy animals. Bears, owls, ducks and rabbits. I didn't have a doll until I had a Sindy, and she bought that begrudgingly. I had to learn my times tables for Sindy, as Mum didn't approve of her. She bought me Tilly in my teens.

The bell went, it was Sami. I half hid behind the door so she couldn't see my tear-stained face. She poked her head around with her big, brown concerned eyes and asked to come in for a bit just to see that I was all right. I let her in and we went to my room, purposefully being quiet so as not to wake Gareth.

After a short time she had me laughing and I forgot the hysterical crying, we always did laugh a lot together. But then I felt shame, my shifting state seemed disrespectful. Then I was filled with fear for when Gareth would wake up. I couldn't be in the house when he did, I couldn't be the one to tell him. Sami said we could go to her house. I got together some things for the night. We walked there, we were chatting normally by then. I wasn't good at being sad in front of others. When we arrived at her house her mother gave me a firm hug. Sami's younger brothers looked at me with sympathy, with a tentative warmth. We went to her room with its ripe cherry Laura Ashley wallpaper that matched her cherry duvet cover that we lay on after school as we giggled and talked together. I wanted to act normally because it was all I could bear to do in that whirlwind of the unimaginable.

When I had told Sami on the phone that morning that Mum was dead, she had immediately called our friends to cancel the plans we'd made for New Year's Eve. I asked her to call them back and say that we should go out as arranged. She did, and when we went out she linked her arm through mine, as I sometimes had with my mother. We drank cheap wine, and it made no difference. The unreal, that fiction, was still nesting.

In the years that followed, New Year's Eve was a double-edged sword. A threatening remembrance of a date in the past, but supposedly also a date when hope could be entertained. The promise of a new cycle, new seasons, of a whole new year and the possibility that implies. If I could just not look back. For the first few years after her death, still wrestling with the numbness, I told myself that everything would be different in each burgeoning year. I thought she might be around at that time, listening to our expectations because it was the anniversary of her death, and an involuntary rite of passage she might want to attend. It wasn't an allocated date to mourn, but one to think of her and to hope that she might be thinking of us.

One New Year's Eve, as I left one pub with my friends to go to another, I bumped into Gareth in the dark street. I asked him if he wanted to join us, he said he'd rather be on his own. Secretly, I was glad as I felt I couldn't cope with him that night. Now I wish I had dragged him with me. We sat on the pavement outside the Steels pub on Haverstock Hill, the chilled night wrapped itself around us. His eyes were sad and lost and lonely. He looked out across the street as if he wanted to find something in the nocturnal London air. Cars whizzed past. Gareth wanted to talk. He kept saying there was no reason to stay alive if this was what life amounted to. It was a routine conversation for us, I said the usual, the ineffective manifesto. Things can and do get better, things change, you may never feel as bad again as you do now. But he didn't absorb my words, he couldn't take them in. He'd heard them for years. If anything, they may have brought home the plain unbearability of it all, because in years things hadn't changed.

Instead, words hurt Gareth. He was dyslexic and felt desperately inadequate because of it. He was insulted by books which contained words he had difficulty reading. Each one mocked him and he became even more distrustful of them. Abrasive letters hovering on a page whose purpose seemed to be to outdo him. Lonely enough to need them, but words cut the wounds deeper instead of soothing. They screeched to Gareth from the page, and didn't appear to do much else when spoken.

That night I wanted to get drunk and he wanted to die, as he did on many nights. He spoke of his recurring sadness over our mother's death, how that was the last straw. When I tried to hug him he gave me the Gareth hug, the one that touches only lightly. It was more than a pat on the back and less than an embrace, but as much as he could do because he was afraid of touch. He had a body made for bear hugs, six foot two and broad, he should have been a great enveloper. He had spoken of this reluctance to touch. He must have been yearning deep inside for the pressing warm skin of others, but he didn't think he was good enough to touch other people. Like a traitor I watched him walk down the dark hill alone and rejoined my friends.

The first night she was dead I slept at Sami's house. I did not believe I would carry on living. I lay in bed trying to imagine five or ten years into the future. I could not. How could I exist if she didn't? I could not foresee a life that wasn't frozen in limbo. I wondered how I would wake the next morning, perhaps I would mysteriously join her from my sleep. Maybe she would come and get her three children because she would want us with her. That night I dreamt she phoned to say she hadn't really died, she just had to go away for a while to rest, but she would come back and it wouldn't be too long to wait until she did.

The next day, I knew I had to go back home and see my family. I called the house and found my father was back from Scotland, his brother was there also. Our uncle had come to support us even though we children hardly knew him. We hadn't yet found Callum, he was surfing on a wave somewhere in Cornwall. Dad had asked the local police to look for him.

I caught the bus home. I dreaded walking into the house. I didn't want to see my family. What could they do? I unlocked and pushed open the door, and a subdued hum reached up to tell me they were in the kitchen. I went downstairs to see them. There were no great hugs, instead there were pathetic hellos, almost muttered under breath. They had already started discussing the funeral arrangements. I feared they would take over her last goodbye, it was the one thing I had left to do for her and they had started without me. I made some feeble comment about making sure that we do what she would have wanted, when of course I didn't know what she wanted for her funeral – she had probably never thought about it. She was only fifty. She hadn't made a will, her own death hadn't crossed her mind, despite death's presence in her everyday life through her son. All I knew was that I couldn't tolerate her body being underground, becoming the gauntlet for worms and insects and all kinds of subterranean life. I asserted that I wanted her to be cremated and no one objected. I also wanted her ashes to be buried rather than scattered so that we would have somewhere to go and visit her. Gareth was quiet, he stayed away from us. I went into the sitting room where he was and asked him how he felt.

'Well, this doesn't exactly help my situation does it?' He didn't know how to express anything else.

I couldn't be around him. I went upstairs to my bedroom and my father came after me. He spoke his sadness, of how awful it was that she had died. I told him she now had peace, which was all I was able to say. He grabbed me, as others came to when they learned of her death. He had me in his arms, tight. I could barely breathe and he was crying, crying for how terrible it was that we no longer had a mother. I, too, wondered how it would be without her.

I cannot recall the days between her death and her funeral. But her funeral I remember well. The four of us – Dad, Callum, Gareth and me – closed the door of our pink house, knowing that when we returned we would have buried her ashes. Our mother had painted the door with roses and vines, with bees buzzing around the two-dimensional foliage. She would paint anything she could get her hands on; walls, furniture or paper. Callum was driving us to her town, Oundle. She had moved to Oundle when she left our house in London because her sister lived there and because it had a swimming pool and a theatre, essential criteria for her.

As we were getting into the car, Dad and Gareth fought over who would sit in the front seat. It was a ridiculous quarrel. As head of the family our father thought he should be sitting in it. Gareth thought he was entitled to it in the same way he thought he was entitled to everything, and because he didn't want to sit next to anybody else. He wanted the room and he wanted the distance from us. Neither one was going to give an inch. Bulls at loggerheads, stubborn as the sun on the desert, as the water which races towards the fall. There was no chance in hell of either one changing his mind. Callum, the most diplomatic of us, tried to reason with both of them in the hope that one would back down. I thought that because Gareth was so impossibly difficult Dad should give the seat to him. Submit, give in for the sake of a bit of peace just as our mother had in every instance, that this should have been avoided on the day of her funeral even if it meant letting Gareth get away with everything as usual. This was not the day to start asserting authority. Maybe my father thought that because it was the day of her funeral was the very reason not to let him get away with it as he always had with her. She would let most things go with Gareth in the quest for an interlude in the tension. Dad wanted to discipline his son, stop him taking advantage of every single situation, prevent Gareth from demonstrating that he was the one who ruled the family, even though he did, by throwing his temper and his physical strength here, there and everywhere. We were all supposed to live with it. Saying no to Gareth usually ended up in subtle acts of violence. He pushed and pushed until it ended in loudness and hurt. Selfishness thrives well in depression. It grows grabbing limbs which see no other way, leeching others of what they have.

For his grand finale, Gareth tried his best to rip the front seat out of the car. The red box rocked as he tore at it. In the end he refused to drive with us and walked off. Callum chased him down the street and gave him money to get there by train. We weren't sure he'd make it, he had a habit of wandering off and not returning for longer than expected. Maybe that fight was an elaborate way of avoiding the funeral he couldn't face.

My father got into the seat which was permanently wonky from then on, and sorted out his hair that had been messed up during the fight. Once we got going the journey was fine.

We drove past fields. Past the smell of cow dung that she had preferred to perfume.

I've inherited her taste for unlikely aromas. In petrol stations and multi-storey car parks I breathe the smell of the fuel deep into my lungs, have done since I was a young child. I would stand by the pumps and take in as much as I could through my nostrils before my mother paid for the petrol and we had to drive off, I reluctantly so. And, even more oddly, I savour the smell of London Underground tube stations. The dusty London fragrance, that gets trapped down there along with the rats, fills me with olfactory pleasure. A bizarre inheritance from her.

We arrived in Oundle. Gareth had made it, too.

That night, before her funeral, I stood before her wardrobe. Beautifully painted by her, it had a full-length mirror. I hoped to see her as I looked into the mirror, her in me, or her come to see me. But it was just me. I took her clothes off their wooden hangers, the rich fabrics she cherished. She would scour jumble sales in her attachment to clothes gone by, for clothes whose previous owners had decided were past their use-by-date.

I smelt them knowing their smell, her smell, would not last. It was the smell of comfort I was losing, of familial intimacy, her scent had long ago come to feel like home. I would recognize it when I discovered it elsewhere, but it would be random, a lucky find if it happens. It might brush past me in a street or a restaurant, but would no longer linger as it had on her.

I pulled over my legs, christened matchsticks by my brothers, her long black skirt. Over my head I dragged her olive green, crushed velvet shirt adorned with flamboyant ruffles, catching the light as velvet does in its squashed finery. They did not fit. Still skinnier and shorter than my mother, the skirt gathered around my feet, the top hung off my narrow build. Brought home to me was my child status. Just because she had gone did not mean I had become an adult. A part of me felt that with her death I should suddenly have grown up.

When I was tiny she made my clothes, often from the unpicked material of her own old clothes. Floral summer dresses with smocking across the front. I remember my impatience for her to complete the intricate stitching because I was longing to wear the dress. She made me a white pinafore, with frills on the skirt and tied up with a bow around my back.

Drowned beneath her clothes, I fantasized about the day when I would be big enough to fit them, the day when I would bear her body, when I would possess my adult female self. In doing this I realized she wouldn't see me as a grown woman. I was the youngest when she died, Callum and Gareth were already tall, already nearly big. I knew then she wouldn't see me doing any of the things grown women do. She had said she was looking forward to being a grand-mother. If I were to carry on her lineage, pass her genes to another, she wouldn't see. Whatever I were to do, she wouldn't see. Sami said she has a ringside seat, but how would I know if and what she chose to watch if I couldn't see her watching?

The last time I saw her before she died was through the square glass window of her hospital room's door, with its criss-cross wire meshing. Her face was divided into lots of tiny squares, as it would be if you were to paint a portrait of her, in preparation for the mimicking of her face. Portrait for the memory. I was about to leave the hospital after a visit and she wanted to see a nurse, I don't remember why. Probably to help her do something she could no longer do herself. As I walked back past her room after asking for a nurse I glanced in, she was sitting up in bed, propped by pillows, looking a little lost, listless and powerless. She was almost without her voice by then. To be soundless is to be vulnerable. It was hard to see her vulnerable.

I remember a fight she and I had when I was twelve. In my adoles-cence, during arguments, I would scream so loudly that the walls and doors would seem to shake. My parents attributed my temper to the fact that I was a redhead. Hair and temperament entwined, a Celtic hand-me-down that was explicable but inexcusable. She and I were standing on the landing outside my bedroom. I don't recall what I was upset about. I yelled and ranted and she hardly fought back. I saw that she could no longer fight, not with me and not with anyone. Her ability and desire to wrestle for what she thought was right and wrong, for what she thought was unacceptable to come out of my mouth, was gone. She was unguarded back then. Her frailty gripped me and I was disgusted with myself because I'd attacked her when she was weak and unable to shut myself up. There, on her face, was the toll taken by everything that had happened to her.

I withdrew to my bedroom, pressed my back against the door, tears of shame dripped. I promised myself I would never again cause her more upset, I would not be the one to contribute further to her anguish. A couple of years later she told me that she didn't know what had caused my hot-headed temper to stop overnight. I just felt different, I told her.

She didn't see me glancing at her through the boxed window in the hospital, she looked into thin air, patiently despondent with her invalidity. This was enforced rest for her, she would never have rested without being taken ill. A woman who would go on until she broke. The look in her eyes as she sat up in that hospital bed – the eyes of a child who needs to be taken care of, to be nurtured until they can stand on their own two feet. The skin and muscles around those eyes had relaxed because she didn't have to be in control anymore. That's the face that comes back to me, one that couldn't any more. I saw her, just as I would later see Gareth through glass built from sand. Grain after grain. Life after life.

The funeral was held in the old church in the centre of her tiny town. We wanted her ashes to be buried there but there was no room left in the graveyard. It's full of bodies from the nineteenth and early twentieth century, leaving no space for modern flesh. There was a place she had taken me to, a clearing in the middle of a forest where every inch was covered by bluebells. It was out of this world, the end of the earth as she would say. My mother had taken me there because she was astounded by its beauty and wanted to share the paradise with me. It was a wonderful thing to do, and nothing like she had ever done before. I wanted her to be buried there but I couldn't remember where it was. I have the most appalling sense of direction and had no idea how to begin to find my way back to it. The dead probably weren't welcome there anyway. Instead she was to be buried in a graveyard next to fields on the outskirts of Oundle. Her final place of rest would be perused by nothing more than cows and a benign view across the countryside.

It was my first funeral. Callum, Gareth and I sat in the front pew. It was strange to be within those four walls, stained glass and stone arches, saying goodbye to Mum, with the knowledge that those were the last moments her body would be around us. The melancholic-looking pallbearers stepped past us with their polished black shoes, shining enough to sparkle beneath her coffin. They held the box up on their shoulders, carried her in death as if she were a dependent child once more. One of them nearly tripped over the carpet in the aisle but managed to regain his composure and her weight. I thought, and I know my brothers did too, that her humour would have warmed to a pallbearer who tripped up, just so long as the cadaver didn't come crashing out before us to intervene with her final dignity.

White lilies and red roses, loads of them, cascaded over the edges of the coffin. My father said lilies were one of her favourite flowers. They symbolize purity, peace and resurrection, regeneration and immortality. To me they were a callous reminder of Dante Gabriel Rossetti's painting of the Annunciation. The scared pale Mary crouches in the corner, shrinking into the wall. She stares at the lily pointed at her womb which tells her she has been impregnated by God's will. The lily speaks more of dread than of miracles of life in that painting. I wished we could have asked my mother what flowers she wanted.

Hymns were sung that my brothers and I didn't know. Dad had chosen them. We weren't christened and we never went to church so we were clueless at her funeral. All the talk of God taking her back into his fold reinforced how she was no longer with us.

I thought about how pretty the church was, of the countless weddings and funerals that had been held there. The dead and the live bodies that had passed through its doors. It wasn't big, we were close, close enough to hear tears dislodge. It must seem odd saying goodbye in massive churches or cathedrals where there is no intimacy even in the final moment. I felt as though I had been placed there by mistake. My presence was an accident. I didn't believe I was there and she was in that coffin and wouldn't be around us again. It was like acting in a play, appearing at a function that you didn't want to attend. Getting on with it, putting in an appearance, being a body that was supposed to be present. There wasn't that much sadness because it wasn't happening. I had a brother either side of me. I felt for them more than anyone else.

After the church service her body was taken away to be cremated. We drove to the graveyard and waited in parked cars for her ashes to arrive. Sat still as she was burnt. They were to be buried in a small wooden box with a brass plaque bearing her details, her name and the dates of her birth and death. *Margaret Anna Gordon. 19th May 1939 – 31st December 1989.* When her remains arrived we walked to her hole in the earth and words were recited to give her to the ground. Then everyone walked away. I wanted to have the last look so I peered down into the hole and my face was reflected in the brass. She must have been taking a piece of me with her, I thought. She could see me.

Then the congregation went to her house, not far from the graveyard, the house I came to at weekends. The house, a 1930s semi-detached, she hadn't been in long enough to redecorate the 1970s decor. She had moved into it about a year before she died. When she and I went to view it we knew as soon as we walked through the door that it was the house for her. She had looked at me knowingly but also with a trace of apprehension that came from no longer being sure that anything could be just right.

'Mum, it's a happy house,' I had said, and she bought it.

There was a finger buffet. We picked at various quiches cut into manageable slices which hung around the dining room. Yellow triangles, redundant for our lack of appetite.

It was January but not so cold, or maybe we couldn't feel it. Some of us were in the garden with the trees whose bark had come off in uneven patches and the wear of the weather had made it look like military camouflage. The garden brought back her fiftieth birthday party seven months earlier. She considered the party a mark of her new life in a new place. She had met lots of people since moving and wanted to bring them into her new home. She made invitations with one of her trademark podgy cherubs adorning the front, inviting people for *superior squidgy cakes and inferior wines.* She was nervous that it wouldn't go well, that not enough people would turn up. The house turned out to be packed and we spilled out into the garden. It was one of the rare occasions I saw her glowing with happiness.

Some people acted like they didn't belong in her house after the funeral, relatives who had hardly seen her over the years, or people who hardly knew us.

My cousin's polyester skirt started smoking because she stood too close to the buzzing orange burn of the gas fire.

Gradually people left. Like us, most had to drive back home to London that day.

The gravestone couldn't be put up for at least six months because the soil had to harden after being disturbed. I wanted to go there, be by her stone, give her flowers and speak to her. It's not how it is in films or in television dramas, where the bereaved go to the grave in the days following the funeral looking dejected and distraught. We had to wait to be by her stone. We had to earn the soil's trust.

Chapter Seven

I became jealous of the aged. How did they get to some ripe old age when she did not? I saw mothers touch their grown daughters' faces and an anger swelled in me. The green hellfire of envy swept from my organs, I wanted what they had. When I saw different generations of women together, first I wanted to scratch their eyes out. Then I wanted to be like them, to be joined by DNA.

I saw pensioners who could hardly move for illness struggling to get on buses, and leaning on their wayward shopping trolleys in supermarkets for support, and a part of me was grateful that she wasn't around to become immobile. I remembered her saying that if she were ever so ill that life was maintained only by cold, hard hospital machines, she would rather not live. My mother had a moral quarrel with such a quality of life. And as a result of her illness, we learnt, if she had not died her mobility may have been restricted. As an artist this would have been intolerable, quite possibly she would not have been able to paint, at least not as she used to. Such facts were supposed to make us feel better. Persuade us that her awful vanishing was best.

She was about to come into her own, and had met someone else since the breakdown of her marriage to my father. I'd met this new man only once before her funeral and knew little about him. We opened the sealed Christmas card she was going to give him. *Thank you for making the last three months the happiest of my life.* The two of them, she and he, had planned to go travelling together when she came out of hospital.

The summer following her death, Callum and I cleaned out her house. Despite her short inhabitation there was a lifetime of stuff to plough through. Two great wooden chests, whose heavy drawers creaked when opened, overflowed with papers, receipts, letters, her artwork, the work of other artists that had been given to her, and work from her student days at Camberwell College of Arts. She had left Central Saint Martin's because, she had said, the women students were only there to find husbands and she wanted to be an artist. She moved to Camberwell to be taken more seriously. Screen prints, sketchbooks and paintings jostled with one another for space.

The hundreds of children's book illustrations from her creative world were deposited there. The mischievous character she had invented who caused chaos wherever he went, Wilberforce the bear, turned the party of a civilized female bear in a frilly pink dress into a massive food fight. In another book he sent a perfectly stacked pyramid of tins of baked beans in a supermarket crashing down. The first to draw and paint the Wombles, all the illustrations she had produced before the television puppets embezzled her vision of them were living there in those wooden drawers, keeping one another company. Gareth was particularly proud of Mum's Wombles. He carried in his caged chest indignation that she hadn't received the recognition for them he felt she deserved. Nudes from the 1960s and 1970s with long yellow flowing locks, curling to the corners of the page, were surrounded by pink and red sinuous swirls and sunflowers. She admired Art Nouveau, the Fauves and Chagall, and in her art she turned these influences elegantly psychedelic. Immaculately crafted traditional oil portraits didn't look like they could be by her, but they were. Lithographs of ships in storms and pretty young girls in straw hats holding flowers were heaped in many different colours. We found illustrations for a book that hadn't been published, the story of a mermaid who was found crying in a dustbin by a young girl named Matilda. Matilda helped the mermaid out of the dustbin and took her on her tricycle to a place of safety in the shade under trees, where she would not dry up. Later she bathed and fed her, as every six-year-old girl should do when she comes across a mermaid. The folk in her art gathered to testify to her imagination. My mother saw many worlds in her head, then spread them out on paper and canvas.

There were ancient oil paints, tubes squeezed out of shape, cracked so the paint would squidge out everywhere but through the top if squeezed once more. She didn't seem to throw much away, even if it was beyond use. There were letters from people we had never heard of, which didn't mean much as our parents knew many, many people. Some seemed intimate beyond a friend's written words, but then again, how dare we assume when we couldn't ask her. One friend sent her a miniature oil painting of a landscape every season. Years of seasons were hoarded, fallen orange leaves, blue and white snow dropping to the ground, buds of flowers aspiring to open and expansive yellow fields dressed by the sun.

Relatives had taken their pick after her funeral. Some of them asked for a couple of pieces of work, but then proceeded to carry away a crowd of her creatures. We packed up the rest of her pictures and the things, her things, we wanted to keep in boxes and put them in the attic. Callum, Gareth or I would retrieve her possessions when one of us owned our own house with enough room for them.

We had decided we would rent out her house, she had bought it so recently it seemed daft to sell it straight away. And we didn't want to let it go just yet, because it was hers.

We were there for a week, looking through her paper history, cleaning and packing. Spirit is embedded in paper molecules, in this archive of life. Each thing we picked up we wanted to savour, internalize, but there was so much to do we didn't have the time to delve deeply, to read all her letters or pore over her art.

What we did look at closely raised questions about her. We knew only the highlights, just meagre facts of her life's chronology, but not the details of her past. Callum was particularly frustrated that we'd never find out about certain things, curiosity couldn't be truly quenched. Since leaving home for university he had begun to know her as a person rather than a mum, and that process had been stopped in its tracks. Her death also made him aware of his own mortality, in part because of her pictures. Despite her dying there was something precious left; harshly, that made him feel that if he died there would be nothing. A few years later, in my late teens and his early twenties, when we travelled a fair bit together, he became an avid photographer and with a pocket-sized palette of watercolours he painted the places we went to. With creativity he embarked on recording our lives.

Her clothes confounded me. I didn't know what to do with them. They were too big for me and no one else wanted them. They wanted her easily wearable jumpers with bright patterns, but not the sheathes of charm, her gear for nights out to boxing matches, the theatre or parties she went to with my father. Maybe they were too uniquely hers. In truth I wanted them, but if I had taken them then I would have been playing dress up. Girl dressed as a woman. I couldn't imagine that I would ever wear such stuff. Her clothes were the finery you break into, like seductive lingerie or stiletto shoes.

I wouldn't have worn them then, and it didn't occur to me I might want them later.

She would rarely buy new clothes despite wearing them well. Her tall, narrow frame was easily flattered by cut cloth. People often commented on how fabulous she looked even though she just mixed around the few clothes she had. On the unusual occasion she did buy something new, as soon as we got home she would hide it at the back of her wardrobe. Her wardrobe overflowing with accumulated stuff. Plastic bracelets and necklaces, strings of fake opulence hanging like temptation. Scarves so sexy I yearned for them as I grew up, wanting to wrap my neck or my shoulders in the glamour of my mother. Sometimes things would sit there for weeks and weeks in plastic bags, as if not wearing it straight away would make it less new and therefore less noticeable when she did eventually allow the item daylight.

My mother felt she shouldn't be spending money and suffered from guilt when she did. She was wary, fearful of money, or rather, the lack of it, and as a result was very careful with it. I must have been eight when she took me to the bank to withdraw cash for a second-hand car she was buying. Her face went white with nerves. I, too, couldn't believe what a few hundred pounds in cash looked like. It was real Monopoly money. She folded the notes neatly and zipped them up safely in her handbag. A heap of printed paper, the Queen's head in pastel colours, settled in the security of how much her head was worth. But Mum was just plain daunted.

When pound coins first appeared she loosened up. She said they looked like chocolate money and therefore it didn't feel as though you were really spending.

Everything went to charity shops, as many dead people's clothes must do. The goods from the jumble sales she had braved, soldiering through the mobs to grab the best cast-offs first. She had spent years acquiring garments she had fallen in love with. Their texture, their life, her life that she grew into them, that they drew from her. But I couldn't bear their burden so they had to go.

Later they haunted me because I wanted them back. I wanted to wear the second skin she had shed. Be dressed by what dressed her.

She always slept naked. She said she couldn't stand the restriction of clothes in bed. When, as a child, I asked for a nightdress, because I was bored of pyjamas, she was reluctant to buy me one because of how knotted up I would feel. After some persuasion we finally made it to C & A, and she bought me two, one pink and one blue. Sure enough, the first night I wore one of them the damn thing writhed all over the place, throughout the night it crawled from my knees to my neck. She, as much as I hated admitting it, was right.

My mother hated underwear as well as night clothes, in particular bras; she called them body scaffolding. But when it came to me buying underwear she relished the frivolity of going through Marks and Spencer's lingerie department. Flat-chested until the age of sixteen, prior to suddenly being faced with a bosom totally out of proportion to the rest of my curveless body, I bought all kinds of stuff that she thought was delectable. Satin camisoles and little lace numbers. This was an indulgence we entertained together in the couple of years before she died. We had fun, it was one of the few times that I saw her getting excited over something just for the hell of it.

Once, when I showed her a picture in a magazine of a model wearing a silvery grey dress barely long enough to cover her backside with a corsage attached to the shoulder strap, to my surprise she said with total self assurance, 'If I was your age I would go straight out and buy that.' In that moment I saw her as a young woman, her younger glamour I'd heard people talk about. And I saw she loved that I was arriving at this point where we could wallow in these things together. It was a time of recognizing that we were both, nearly, women. Though our relationship was still not without ambivalence. I was so alienated from her that I couldn't speak to her about certain matters I would have hoped to. I didn't tell her I'd started menstruating because I thought she might regard me with confusion and perhaps distaste.

Sorting everything out in the height of a half-decent English summer was hard work. To reward ourselves Callum and I took our bikes and pedalled to nearby towns. We picked berries along the way and bought eggs from farms. For a week we swathed ourselves in the land she had lived in. We cycled for miles on open stretches of road surrounded by fields. The more we rode the more we were able to get done when we returned to her house, and we would keep going, submerging ourselves in another batch of stuff which needed to be organized, late into the night.

Callum and I had spent little intensive time together when younger, and it was during this spell in her house that we started to become close and protective of one another. Though emotions were almost blocked out – they had to be as we had much to do in little time – we were gaining a sense of our new-found state as bereaved siblings. He was encouraging, he pushed me to keep going when I thought I couldn't do anymore, as he would later in life whenever I felt I had run out of steam. And he made being in her house feel fine because he found it comforting even though she wasn't there.

Invading her solitude felt fraudulent. I wanted information about her, but didn't want to rummage through her private possessions. Then again, we couldn't throw things away or store them blindly without first looking at them. How much respect one pays to privacy after someone's death is awkward and clumsy. It is harder to walk away than it is to filter through their belongings. Even though it is, in part, an empty exploration. Whatever you find and want to know more about, questions will stay unanswered, confuse you further in your deeper recesses. The thought that someone will go through my things after I die is hideous to me. It leaves you stripped bare with no room for a private mind – not if you wrote, drew and received letters. But worse still is to leave people lost, with nothing to go on, no thoughts documented, no history to survive you.

I was seeing my mother for the first time as we went through her remaining world. I saw her creative life, her self away from us. We never would have scrutinized her in this way were she still alive. I knew what she did and I knew she was good at it, but I hadn't *looked* at all her art, and seen her psyche in it.

Every day when I came home from school I saw her working. She was there at her table in front of the window painting away. I'd tread down the steps to the basement door and as I walked in she would peer over what she called her granny specs, lower them till they dropped to the end of her neat nose and say hello. She would sometimes draw me when she needed a little girl to be in an illustration for a book. Once, she gave me an orange and told me to pretend it was a donut and sketched me sitting on one of our dining room chairs. My matchsticks with my fallen down socks dangled above the floor. As she began to draw a sumptuous donut filled with jam and cream in place of the orange I was holding, I thought I'd been hard done by.

At night, Callum and I took turns to cook. It felt as though we were kids messing about in a kitchen we weren't supposed to be in, because it wasn't ours, it was hers. It was one thing to be there when she was, quite another when she was wasn't.

I stood motionless in the kitchen knowing she was the last person to use everything. It was a paralysing thought, I was about to desta-bilize her deserting presence. I could have moved things to where she would never have placed them. I could have used something that was not supposed to be used. The last cup of tea in the cup by the kitchen sink was drunk by her. With a magnifying glass I could have traced the marked waves of her sipping lips on the rim of the cup. The plates that were hardly ever used were placed at the back of the cupboard with her hands, covered with her fingerprints. How long would it take to erase every one of her prints from the house? How many times would it be cleaned before there was no physical trace left? Hairs that had dropped from her head were around, lying on the carpet waiting to be hoovered up. Surely we must have missed stuff as we cleaned, she must have stayed for a while. I could have dusted the house for her prints, had her paws around me for a while longer, recorded her scent like a hunter, proved that she was there all along. I could have followed a sequence of her movements, known where she had last been.

I cooked chicken in breadcrumbs, just as she had made it.

When she was living with us she cooked it every Saturday night. Chicken and chips. She soaked her chips in water for hours before cooking them, which is apparently the secret of the best crispy chips. We would eat one after the other because she sliced the chicken so thinly that only enough for one person would fit in the frying pan, and she didn't want us eating lukewarm food that had gone soggy in the oven.

She loved to cook and she was amazing at it. Grand roasts, Indian curries, Chinese dishes, lasagne cooked as only Italians make it, crêpes filled with chicken concoctions, beef stews left to cook slowly so that the meat was unbearably succulent, pizzas made from the recipe of the pizzeria in London where she and my father ate in the 60s when they were courting. Her flair for cooking was best divulged in her desserts which we were treated to at weekends: Black Forest gateau, ginger ice cream with stray chunks of stem ginger to be haphazardly found, the creamiest strawberry ice cream which was a luscious pink, a pink you might want to be swallowed up by, peppered with strawberry seeds, a bitter gooseberry sorbet, vanilla ice cream that was really vanilla and not synthetically plain like the stuff from ice cream vans, Chinese toffee apples that were amazing when they worked, though the toffee didn't always go hard, meringue cake with coffee cream filling and fine chocolate grated on top, profiteroles dripping with dark chocolate sauce, brandy snaps bulging with cream delicately stacked on a plate, chocolate truffles dipped in bitter cocoa, and rich chocolate mousse set in old wine glasses.

On the morning of my seventh birthday, when I walked into our dining room there was a cake on the table with three peach-coloured ballerinas pirouetting on top. There was a huge ribbon tied around it. This cake was so perfect to me, at that time I was an up and coming prima ballerina, that I did not believe my mother's hands could have crafted it. The icing was impossibly smooth and the ribbon full and flouncy. Surely cakes like this only came from masterful bakers? I repeatedly asked her if she had really made my dancing cake, but she had no interest in defending her talents.

Our dining room table was an oak oval, sunk into the floor with spiralling legs. She wiped it with malt vinegar and some other mysterious liquid every day, leaning across the width of the table in vast swooping stretches with a cloth. She said you have to feed the wood or it will starve and the rich colour would disappear.

Now the table needs to be worked on, nurtured from decay back to its former state. It is scratched where someone didn't care, and the deep, resonant colour of the wood has faded to an unvarnished, naked covering.

We had William Morris wallpaper on our dining room walls, printed tropics, virile gardens for the British. I think those crawling flowers were real for her. This paper changed twice. It was green when I was born, and then it turned blue when the green turned tatty. A similar print, a different colour. How quickly after it was put up it became claustrophobic. Changing a colour doesn't change the house. My mother was a fan of Morris. Even when she left and moved to her new house in an old town, she stitched curtains from Morris fabric for the French doors in the dining room. The colour was lighter though, pretty for longer. A beige, almost dusty pink. It was a flesh-like colour, warm flesh, not a cold shoulder like the blue of our dining room walls.

Callum and I ate her chicken and chips on her table with the darkness of her garden shut out by her beige flowers. My version of her recipe was somewhat crisper, blacker, and the kitchen was smoked out, but still it was a taste of her.

When my mother was twenty she burnt her arms and legs in a cooking accident. She was making a meal at a friend's house. The chip-pan caught fire and she, to stop the kitchen setting on fire, valiantly picked up the burning pan and carried it out into the garden. The flames whooshed back on to her, she dropped the pan and her nylon stockings melted onto her legs.

She was taken to Lewisham Hospital where her various burnt bits were bandaged. She stayed there for several weeks. Her fingers were dressed separately so they didn't grow webbed, and one of her legs was put into a cage to protect it. She was scarred from her wrists to her upper arms and slightly on her neck, with raised water-like ripples. She didn't seem to care too much about the burns, yet she always wore long sleeved t-shirts, jumpers and dresses. Her arms were only seen when she swam or was washing.

At the time of the accident, instead of having skin grafts, to treat the burns she was given a drug that was still undergoing research. When she died her sister wondered if that mystery drug had anything to do with her fatal illness thirty years down the line. Searching always for a reason.

I decided that her burnt arms were those of the phoenix who rose from the ashes, who would rise in a second life and fly above her first burning.

When I was small things were said by my ten-year-old friends that made me feel protective of my mother. Sometimes they said things I didn't understand, other times they were shocked that she did or didn't do certain things.

One weekend, four of us went to stay at a cottage in Norfolk belonging to a friend's family. We slept in two bunk beds in a tiny room. We were so close that you could hear our breathing as if we were in one bed, and the heat that escaped from our bodies quickly steamed up the tiny square window.

When we rose the following morning Amy asked to brush my hair. She began brushing it gently, after a while she started brushing the underneath. She found what I had accepted as if it were an organic part of my body, a huge matted knot of hair, tight and built up resting on the nape of my neck. They kept asking, 'Why didn't your mum brush it out?' They implied she was odd because she didn't groom me as their own mothers did. She would make a few brisk strokes on the outer layer of my hair so that it looked neat and tidy, never detangling the underneath, then send me off to school. The only way to get rid of the knot was to cut it out. Amy took scissors to my hair and removed this chunk of mess. From then on I started brushing my own hair everyday.

Since we were little our mother had washed our hair, one after the other, in one of the two stainless steel sinks in our kitchen. I dreaded it, would do anything to get out of it and feigned utter confusion that the time had swung around again. Hadn't we just had our hair washed? But standing there with a bird's nest perched on top of my head, she was uninterested in my poor attempts at lying. Once she had us into position, standing on a chair we'd stretch our necks like ostriches and drop our heads forward into the water and she would briskly shampoo our riots of hair, our heads bobbing back and forth and side to side as she did so. Next she would towel dry our hair and rub the wet right out, shaking our heads vigorously. After years of hating this saga I suddenly stopped fighting hair-washing day. She scrubbed our heads roughly and out of the blue the strength of her hands on my scalp felt good. The touch of her felt good.

She cut our hair until we were in our early teens. She laid out newspaper on the kitchen floor and sat us one by one on a chair in the middle of it, she worked around us with the large silver scissors she used for her artwork. She kept locks of the hair she had cut in envelopes that were then put in files with our names on. Later when I went through these files I witnessed my hair's progression from blonde, to orange, to red. The article that had appeared in the *Evening Standard* about babies being induced was in the file too. She had been interviewed because I was induced, she said she didn't care how her babies were born as long as they were healthy. The accompanying photo showed my bemused, squashed, baby face held close to her soft face with its gentle, uncertain smile.

The year after she died I went to her hairdresser, a snipping woman my mother praised highly. For years she had gone to a hairdresser who spent hours fiddling about, as she had put it, bringing her cups of well-brewed tea and checking that the music humming in the background was to her liking. It was the kind of tinkering, twitching time wasting that Mum found intolerable, and she never much liked the result of the haircut, saying she felt somewhat like a badly sheared sheep. Then she found this gifted scissor lady who charged less than half as much and did it in less than half the time.

When I sat in the hairdresser's chair I imagined her placing her hands and scissors on my mother's hair. The way hairdressers run their fingers through your hair and hold it out to the sides to decide how much to cut off. The way they shampoo your tresses in those sinks that nearly cripple your neck regardless of how much they alter them. She did to me what she'd done to her. Her chopped off hair had dropped on that floor, as mine did.

Once grown from the root, hair is dead. That means hairdresser's floors are akin to butcher's floors, dead matter here and there around our feet.

One day, while Mum was talking to another mother outside the school gates, my friend Amy, the discoverer of my knot, said to me, 'Your mum's a nervous wreck you know.' It wasn't a question.

'I know,' I said. But truthfully I had no idea what she was saying, and she didn't say it nastily. With this declaration she was almost tender, sorry for me. Just matter of fact, crystal clear, Mum was a nervous wreck. She must have heard her mother talking or other mothers gossiping.

That same night I climbed up to Callum's room at the top of the house. His room was the best out of our three bedrooms because it opened out onto the balcony, the balcony that allowed Jelly and I to talk at night when her parents thought she was asleep, her bedroom was at the top of their house. We experimented with various forms of communication before sticking to good old-fashioned talking. Walkie-talkies which were practically useless, you couldn't hear anything unless you were less than three metres apart. We tried setting up strings and ropes where we could shoot notes to one another in a tin carrier. The only problem being that her house was slightly lower than mine, so I never received any replies to my messages.

Callum spent a lot of time in his room, making and creating things. If he wasn't intricately painting a whole army of Dungeons and Dragons figures, creatures from fantastical magic lands, he was building castles out of paper, or making a papier mâché mountainous empire across the length of his bedroom wall.

He studied hard, too. Often, when I went up there he had his head in books. I would wish that I was higher up in school so I could study as hard as him. That night I hung around long enough to ask him what a nervous wreck was.

'Why, do you think that's what Mum is?' he replied to my question.

'No,' I said, 'I just wondered what one was.'

He didn't give me an explanation.

For years after she died I ran. On planes, trains and buses, suspended in moments of perpetually leaving. When I was eighteen Callum asked me if I wanted to travel to India with him and I said yes without even thinking, I just wanted to leave. Once there, the travelling was more important to me than where we ended up. Spending three days on a train or a day and a night on a bus was perfect, as long as I was moving.

I was convinced transience was my only hope of sanity. If I wasn't in one place, if I was in between, I was fine. Not faced with a place, no static position, I believed if I ran things would get better, they had to if I was somewhere else. When I got somewhere, when I stopped travelling, I was dumbfounded. Didn't know what to do with myself. I wanted to keep on moving, but I didn't know where to, or how, because I was tired.

In England, after Gareth died, I ran to the sea because it returned to me the breath I was gasping for. A violent thunderstorm hailed on a lost ability to feel. That sound of pelting drops revived me from a lost, rank, place.

125

The sea crashing in the night made me realize there was life left in me even if others died. I knew I would not be taken away unless I chose to join it, elected to ride its waves, sate the foaming hunger. The sea swept salt over my tears, seized them for itself. The harsh wind pulled back my hair and froze my scalp, senses stirred from their coma and my wet face told me I hadn't gone under. It flows and breaks regardless of our lives, it wants for no one's misery nor happiness.

The wash on the shore is the sea monster's shaving foam. The stones are drawn back, eaten up as the next wave prepares for its fall. The cunning strength of water, to go in two directions at once. If it can relentlessly have such force, I could keep going. It was my resuscitation, my emergency room. It does not flail, it is calm and peaceful or active and abrupt, an uproar of power. But never does it cease to be.

Months after her death, in rage, in anger at my mother for leaving, I decided to throw away the books she had illustrated and her wedding dress, the only item of clothing of hers I had kept. I ran down the stairs digging my nails into the dense fabric and shoved the dress under my father's nose. He was standing on the landing.

'Do you want this?' I said aggressively.

'What is it?'

I dashed past him without giving him an answer, furious that he didn't recognize the deep purple velvet knee-length dress with frills on the wrists and hem. She had made it herself on her Singer sewing machine, knowing just how she wanted it to be. I was livid, felt I might explode. Inside I had erupted. A heightening of grief. Was I more enraged at her or at him for not seeing, how could he not realize what it was? Let's throw her away then, be done with her, I thought. The loss. The abandonment. The rejection. I would discard her, as she did us when she died.

Into a skip outside our house I chucked away the threads and seams that had touched her, borrowed her to fill them out. Soon there was rubble from building work across the road on top of the dress. It was buried deep beneath the dirt. Dirt defying beauty. I flung her books on top of it. For some reason I decided to keep her handbag and all the junk that filled it, for a while anyway. Paper whose edges had shrivelled with time and condensation. Her worn-out, red, leather purse, with each snappy click shut of it I fantasized I was out shopping with her. Part of me wanted to lose that too, be completely rid of her. Good riddance to Mum. But I couldn't go that far, couldn't quite eliminate her.

When I told Jelly what I had done she immediately talked to her parents and like rescuers they dug out her books. They said the wedding dress was too deep to reach. Even if they had managed to get to it, it would have been ruined.

I don't know her voice. She is silent. I can imagine the voices of others who have gone, presume to hear what they would have said. But she is a mute. I can't remember what her voice sounds like. I ask her to speak to me but she is hushed. When I think I do hear her, and she is muffled, I do not believe it's her because I don't know how she speaks to me. Others come and go, she stays barred from me.

When I was ten, I went to a summer camp with school friends. For the first time I missed her, and most fearful for me was that I couldn't recall her face. Nothing, not one single feature. I didn't know what she looked like. I thought I wouldn't recognize her when she came to pick me up at Victoria coach station. All week I fretted that I would never see her again because I would be unable to pick her out from the crowd. She would be lost to me forever in a sea of strange faces. I rallied every effort in me to summon her looks, but my will didn't obey. I must not have retained the visual. I could remember what she felt like. It was warm to sit on her lap and lean into her. She was thin but soft to sit on, it was comforting to be upon her. I knew she was kind of blonde, becoming dirty blonde as the years walked by, but that face of hers was missing, nowhere to be found in my child's mind.

As the coach pulled into the terminal I scanned the parents waiting to pick up their children. There she was. I did recognize her. Standing in her long, blue-grey coat, like the ones 1940s resistance fighters wear in films. That's her face, I thought to myself, and engraved it, stuck it with glue to the insides of my skull. I didn't tell her I'd forgotten her face, I was just glad to see her. It has not left me since. It occupies a permanent place, more reliable than different photographs which morph a person's appearance if you are unsure of what they look like, but her voice resists presence.

After her death, years passed and a great confusion unfolded in me, bred and spread weeds resistant to excavation. Eventually I came to realize that I hardly knew her and could no longer make up who and how she was, which her death had enabled me to do. When she was alive I longed for her, like a potential lover you fail to seduce. When she died I thought I had her, because I could fake the memory, filter away her numbness. But my recollections were in part fabricated – I saw she and I going out, cooking, eating, seeing films and driving together more than we had, in fact, done. Never did I exhume conversations, because there were too few to find. I detested this admission, because it meant she could not be an angel to me. I had taken off her wings.

One day, when I was about seven, when Dad came home from work I ran to him. I adored my father. I looked behind me to see if she was watching, I wanted her to see that I would give him affection because she had given me none. We were on the landing,

I scrambled onto him and wound my legs around him. As I climbed up him he tried to put down the manuscripts he was holding. He was hot, beads of perspiration trickled down his lined forehead and I could smell coffee on his breath. My hands around the back of his neck touched his thick dark hair. It was summer and, a sun-worshipper, he was brown. He put me down as he took off his coat. I turned and looked down the stairs to see what she was doing, if she was looking. She was fussing in the kitchen, he went downstairs to her and they talked. I had failed to even catch her eyes.

I had yearned for her to notice me. In my early adolescence I put on make-up. Discovering the realms of make-up will bond me with her, I thought. I went into her bedroom, she was in bed with wine and it was early. I wanted her to be excited over me, her daughter. She said, 'You look like a ghost,' and turned away. White powder on pale skin had made me a phantom not a geisha.

There was a period when I had her. I'm not sure how old I was. For no reason that I was aware of, she started coming into my room at night once I was in bed and sat and talked to me for ten or twenty minutes. This was precious to me. I can't recall what we talked about, just that we did. That ritual was the first closeness associated with her that I remember. There must have been others but I have blanked them, undone them from my reach. Her nightly visits went on for days, maybe weeks. I would have her for a little time every night. And then, without warning, she stopped coming. She was there and then she wasn't, she walked right out before we'd begun.

After losing her came the loss of him.

Giles, with Gareth and Callum, photographed by Fay Godwin

Chapter Eight

We find the suicide's decision hideous. Hideous because their desperation hurts even after they are gone, it ricochets into the night for the living to be hit. How selfish to be someone who can't let go. They've gone, they wanted to go, so let them. The logic rings in my ears like many tiny, stabbing knives.

I am torn between respect for Gareth's decision to placate the intolerable, and the knowledge that his pain may have passed though it seemed it never would. Yet to vilify him for going prevents a peaceful memory of him. That he died by his own hands was not a sin, not scandalous, but a tragedy. Some may have to be allowed to go. But what if we let people go with ease? Do doctors and carers let things slide when it becomes clear that certain people are more determined than others? What if we let them go when perhaps they could have been given a better chance, been fought for harder? What if they change their mind when it is too late? What if in a different moment they would have made a different choice? Questions designed to drive you insane.

I run again, across different oceans and for longer. In Spain, as I ride the bus from the north to the south, dust cooked by the sun rises in the heat, the light glows with the placid fever of the Mediterranean terra. The roads aren't flat and I rise and fall. I am briefly content, most calmed like this, now that Gareth is gone.

Being on the move sets me free. It hands me an anonymity from their deaths. Where I go people don't know and I don't have to think about the dead and the lives they left behind. And then I come back to England and the questions remain the same.

Gareth is perplexing. He divulged lots of his mind and nothing too. He talked all the time about his ailments, but never was an explanation for them found. Everyone involved with him has a different version, physiological, psychological or spiritual. Often people who saw him didn't believe in the last person's treatment, but no doctor or carer made him well.

A straightforward diagnosis, if there is such a thing, never surfaced. In the last years of his life there was a rumour that he had a subtle form of schizophrenia, that if they had known which type they would have been able to control it through medication. Though it did turn out to be just a rumour, he wasn't schizophrenic.

He rattled with drugs, but their effectiveness seemed dubious. Gareth wasn't happy about filling himself with prescribed narcotics. He wanted to know what each capsule, pill or tablet did, and unless he had sufficient information he would refuse to take them. If someone had told him a drug would take away his pain, he wouldn't have thought twice about it, but because he didn't feel substantially different on them, he was reluctant to keep pouring the synthetic hits into his body. They never seemed to do what they were supposed to, or at least, they didn't make him well. But still he was plied with all those drugs, dressed up in their coloured coatings, waiting to be invited into the mouths of the sick. Though of course we don't know how he would have been without them.

Does it make much difference what he had and why he had it? Was it some ancestral root we have within us that could at any moment make us turn upon ourselves? Cognitive processes sabotaged. Trapped in a head that malfunctions. A plethora of chemicals wreaking havoc on our brain and behaviour.

The body of my mother's Uncle Edward was found after he'd gassed himself in 1933. He was twenty-four, the same age as Gareth when he died. When Edward was a baby his brothers and sisters were pushing him in his pram down a hill when they accidentally let go and he fell out and bumped his head. The story goes he suffered from then on.

I read books on schizophrenia and manic depression. Looking for Gareth in the pages. I don't think I find him but no two books say the same thing other than it often has a genetic basis. I am in a maze, blind to what I'm scared might happen.

Statistically, in a family where one suicide has occurred, another will follow sooner or later across generations. It is an act that rears its ugly head amongst the same pool of genes.

We should know how close it is to us, procure acquittal for our souls. Know what to watch for if it calls, comes knocking at the hour when we might be easily eroded. This monster may plague us. Be weaved into our cells waiting to bite with an unexpected poison. Nothing is more hereditary than afflictions of the brain, the grey mush sitting between our ears could double-cross us at any moment. If I don't suspect it, it will happen I assume, catch me unawares. What if this thing whispers to me, reveals itself with open arms without my awareness, takes me on an unwanted winding journey. Abducts me and leaves me in a place I don't want to be. The place where he was. Wretched.

Am I going crazy? Is this grief or a piece of what he had?

I console myself, and know that my ability to do this means I haven't yet left. I don't drown as he did, it doesn't last like his, doesn't consume like his. Rarely do I lose the will to live. I can exploit logic to want to stay alive. He never could.

When I was a young child Gareth's behaviour was generally aggressive towards me so I found it hard to differentiate between his standard ups and downs and his suicidal ups and downs. Though the extent varied, his depression and anger were absolutely consistent. Gareth's behaviour grew to be an entity that was lived with but never deciphered nor understood.

Occasionally the magnitude of his difficulties would be made obvious, his problems made concretely apparent by the intervention of a hospital, clinic or doctor. There was the odd occasion when I would answer the door to a doctor who had come to speak with Gareth and probe his mind for what might be going on in there, for the lurking toxic gremlins. To discern what was making him so melancholic. I remember the knitted jumper one doctor wore. It looked too small for him, maybe it had shrunk in the wash. I peeked around the banisters and down the stairs to see what was going on, nothing much happened. Gareth sat at the kitchen table. An attempt at conversation by the standing doctor gained barely a response from Gareth who looked down, wilfully avoiding the eyes living above the jumper. I think in the early days of his troubles my mother hoped a chat with the doctor might edge her son away from the track he was travelling on, praying that such authority might have clout with his head.

I decide that I will read Gareth's hospital notes. I want to find out what the doctors and psychiatrists thought, what they diagnosed, how they treated him, how they thought they could make him better, and if they ever did think they could make him better. I want to know what went on, what was written about him by the professionals that surrounded him. I want to make sense of it.

Under the Access to Health Records Act 1990, a patient, or a relative of a deceased patient, is entitled to make a formal enquiry to see the notes written about him or her. The wall between medicine's governors and its recipients has weakened over time. I call the hospital to see if I can have access. There are criteria, potential constraints, they could say no if they wanted to. 'Yes, I don't see why you wouldn't be able to read them. We'll write to you with confirmation that you can have access and then we'll arrange for someone to go through them with you.' But I receive no letter. Nothing, confirmation or otherwise. I know how busy, how under-staffed and overworked they are, and I am trying to live without being dominated by Gareth now that he is gone. I do not persist. Maybe someone is being gentle with me, protecting me, doesn't think I should see. Maybe it's best if I don't know.

Nearly five years pass. I still want to know, still want to make sense of it. It eats away at me. What might be there, what answers are bound in those files? There are many blanks and I want to tie it all together, stitch it so it might become a tale with a clearer narrative. I call again. I am passed from one person to another through officialdom and back again. Each in turn blames bureaucracy and says that someone else must be the one to authorize access. I feel they are being obstructive. I write a letter saying that I will ask my solicitor to handle the matter as there is obviously some kind of problem. Finally the request is approved.

I go to the hospital to read the summaries of Gareth. Up the spiral steps that are as familiar to me as the steps of the house we were brought up in. The hairdresser's opposite the hospital has changed its name and decor since I was last there. Much in the area has changed, though the Royal Free feels the same. The hospital staff are benign, kind, and nice to me. They don't fight me like those on the phones did. They offer me tea and they give me a room in which to read the notes alone. I thought there would be boxes and boxes, but there are just two bulging files of paper bound together with an overstretched elastic band. They are divided into years: *Pre 1993* and *Post 1993*. His number is on the front, 'Case History Investigations, Hospital Number: 132892'. The dissection of Gareth lies before me on this vinyl-topped table.

The rest of us have passports, driving licences, cards and diaries. Private letters that tell our lives. We are spread out on different pieces of paper like butter spread naked on toast. Some secret, some not so secret, papers hold us. Our truths, our lies, our own and other people's versions. This is the stuff we want when someone dies. When they leave without telling, without clearing up, without leaving a tidy life.

As I begin to read I hear a disturbance in the corridor. There is banging, a patient is flipping out and staff are trying to calm him. It dawns on me how far removed I have become from this life.

I graze the notes. My head begins to thump, my vision blurs. Simultaneously I want and don't want to read these papers. Initially I cannot be thorough, it is overwhelming. It is too much to have him reduced to professional summations. Mountains of sentences that collect words about him as though he were a specimen under observation, which of course he was. A grim anthology of a finished life. They take me back to parts of my childhood I had forgotten.

Flicking through them, I see that we were also observed. Watched when we came to see Gareth. Less so me, I was the youngest. *His sister is a small, quiet, immature girl.* If we were relevant enough to be looked at, why didn't they talk to us? Years later, when I was less small and my mother was dead, when Gareth returned to hospital they spoke with Callum, but never me. This sparse, restrained communication confuses me. We lived with him, in a family they deemed to be in *serious trouble*. Small maybe, but not mute.

The descriptions of Gareth's difficulties go back to before he was born. To before his skin hit air. *Gareth is described as being always a difficult boy i.e. since birth and even during Mrs Gordon's pregnancy with him.*

The difficult boy. The hard pregnancy. There was a tall story that he'd fractured one of my mother's ribs while she was pregnant with him because he kicked so hard. Like an alien waiting to strike, bursting forth with never-ending cries. An angry and sad spirit. If he had turmoil in the womb, enough to hurt his life-sustaining mother, chances are he would have disharmony out of it. The tale came to take on some resonance.

He was such a pretty baby, with blond locks curling into his face, that admiring broody women would crouch and peer into his pram. They'd smile at Gareth then tilt their heads up to our mother and ask how old she was. I don't know if she bothered telling them Gareth was a he and not a she.

I read what the experts wrote about us. One doctor sent a letter to another on 20 February 1984. I had turned ten five days before and Gareth had just taken his first overdose. The doctor outlined the background of Gareth's prototypical suicide attempt, of his initiation into the mindset which searches for death.

They had already broken off a therapeutic contact with the Department for Children and Parents, of the Tavistock Clinic, who were left knowing there was very serious trouble in the family and hoping that the Gordons would find their way to some clinic before an actual tragedy occurred.

We have only been involved with the family for a few weeks, at the moment it looks as though they will go on working with us because they have now been able to make it clear that the long-term close but pathological relationship between Gareth and his mother, with father standing aside, is breaking down in a way which makes it actually dangerous for Gareth and his mother to try to live in the same place.

We were down as a tragedy waiting to happen.

Callum and I were separated from this triangle. He was a loner, I waited in the wings and watched.

I feel my family has no right to me. They confused, neglected, let love be lost, left us to our own devices.

I recall us going for family therapy. I was taken out of school for the morning and told by my mother that we were going somewhere for a kind of meeting. We drove there, all of us together to this mysterious appointment. In the corridors of the clinic were brightly splashed paintings, presumably to occupy the vision of the young-sters who were there reluctantly. The five of us and two therapists sat in a room in a circle. No one said anything for several minutes. Things were never talked about at home, so how could we talk about them here? The dull grey carpet in the middle of the circle became fascinating to look at. One of the therapists encouraged my mother to speak. She burst into tears as soon as she opened her mouth and nothing was said by anyone. We children continued to look down at the ground, embarrassed to see her crying. We weren't tactile, we couldn't run to her and comfort her. Doing so would have meant tearing away from the only bodies we knew. We were paralysed. The shrill silence. We didn't return as a family.

I read discrepancies between how things felt at home and what the doctors write, what they describe. They missed the subtle points you'd assume they'd catch. They document little that I recognize. They didn't see how Gareth was. They didn't see how Mum was. They didn't know. They were never there.

Early on, I see, doctors advised our parents to keep potentially damaging objects away from us. From his first overdose onwards, Gareth's chosen method of bodily destruction was a bottle of pills washed down with apple juice, followed by a decent bottle of red wine pilfered from our father's cellar. Only later, briefly, glinting razors were his playthings. The shining call of a cut-throat piece of metal.

We suggest that you should find time to discuss the availability to the children of dangerous things such as medicines and razor blades.

And we three children were embroiled in their prognosis.

Did they think we followed like sheep?

I took my overdose when I was thirteen. I calculated the amount of aspirins I would need by comparing my body weight with Gareth's. I needed nothing like as many, but he never succeeded, therefore I needed more. I had no idea what would happen to me. I just wanted to go away for a while, a long time, go into a hibernation that would last beyond the winter. Be less lost somewhere quiet. I expected the effect to be almost immediate, as it is when you have a headache and take aspirin. After taking the pills I was fine for a number of hours, so many hours that I thought nothing was going to happen. I even started to think that, impossibly, my body was stronger than Gareth's despite our difference in size and strength.

I took the bus to Sami's house where I had planned to stay the night. I often slept at her house so that night was nothing out of the ordinary. Her mother cooked spaghetti and two sauces, a tomato sauce and a sauce made of garlic and butter. On Sami's advice I ate the garlic sauce on my pasta.

After dinner I started to throw up. The vomiting became more and more violent. I was up all night, my insides hurling down the toilet. No one could understand it because we had all eaten the same food and everyone else was fine. Sami and her mother looked after me, held my hair back as I threw up, something Sami would come to do with unconditional grace as we got older and started drinking ourselves into sickly states.

The next morning her mother telephoned mine who thought I was lying, playing sick to get off school, as Sami and I had been known to do. One year we got out of doing every single physical education class by forging notes from our mothers. She picked me up from Sami's house, mistrust secreted from her quietly furious eyes. She drove me back home with my head hanging out of the car window, I needed the breeze on my skin, air, not the smell of the car.

We pulled into a petrol station to fill the car up, and the petrol fumes which I would usually have savoured made me retch my guts some more. Then she started looking worried, maybe I wasn't such a cheat after all.

We got home and I clambered pathetically into my squeaky bed with its sagging mattress, and she put a bowl beside me. We always used the same bowl when one of us was sick. It was a foul pink colour, just what you don't want to be faced with when you are ill. I threw up for three days. My stomach was painfully strained from the vomiting and I looked skeletal.

Towards the end of what was deemed to be an inexplicable sickness, Callum came into my room and asked if I was all right. He joked that I was even more of a stick insect than I had been before and said he would now call me Card, short for Playing Card, as when I turned sideways I'd disappear.

When I stopped being sick and started eating again we decided that I must have had gastroenteritis.

The first night I ate was paradise, just to be able to keep something down. My mother gave me a little fish and apple juice, then vanilla ice-cream which was incredibly soothing as it slid down my weary throat without effort. She was worried I'd overdo it and eat too much. But having escaped the jeopardy of my self-induced illness, I was hungry. I knew I was lucky not to have been taken by those who prowl, waiting for the ones that fall. There was something about escaping death, even though I'd manufactured the danger myself, which leaked life back into my veins like oil spreading through a clapped-out engine.

Trying and failing ended my thoughts of how to get to another place where things might be different. From that time I no longer lay in the bath at night wondering how to vanish. Or at least until they died. With Gareth's first attempt, my innocence was irrevocably tarnished, sullied, because I realized that what my mind had been suggesting to me all that time was a desire to leave the body by killing it.

Our mother in particular was under surveillance when she visited the hospital to see her son. The notes say that she suffered from depression and was *somewhat neurotic and dishevelled*. Until I read the observations made of our family I didn't realize the appearance of patients and their families required acknowledgement. The accusation of dishevelment makes my blood rise. Heat rushes through me as I read this, burnt by flames of incredulity. How is one supposed to look when visiting your son in hospital after he has tried to kill himself?

Gareth, who looked just like any other teenager, was *casually dressed in jeans and T-shirt, looking scruffy*. Did they want him in a suit, maybe her too? Is business attire to be donned for psychiatric wards?

Perhaps they should hand out uniforms to new patients as they did in the old days. All the better to make them behave, keep them in line, make them look like each other. Weave them into institutionalized conformity. One nut the same as any other nut, no differentiation between patients.

They say they jot this kind of thing down in the notes because the way a patient dresses reflects his or her state of mind. I don't recall the staff conveying such a smart image themselves, casual is how their guise is best described. To me it was they who tended to appear dishevelled.

Mum did endure depression. Seeing it in writing pays homage to what was easily sensed over the years but never spoken of. To read of her depression is like finding an insightful definition of an allusive word, having an explanation land in your lap that begins to clear things up. The doctors had asked Gareth about his family's mental history. His response is decipherable in the barely legible black and white squiggles designed to be unreadable by a curious third party, as though these papers are secret scriptures. Scribbled by law but never intended to be read.

... He says that none of his family has had any psychiatric history apart from his mother whom he feels at times might have had depression.

I wonder if my mother and brother talked about it, this miserable bond between them. Locked in by one another's pain.

These reams of observed history unwrap the confused thoughts and memories I've had about my mother following her death. I flitted between wanting to keep her, rejecting her, wondering, and then fearing I was like her.

I don't know how much she suffered, it could have been a low hum of deadness or intense periods of clinical depression – unreachable. To me, she was quite simply not there. There in body but with spirit lagging, way behind, left in the distance like a fading shadow. Always, other things were on her mind. The lack of engagement was in the deadness of her expression. So I tried to ignore her absence.

When going about errands we would walk together arm in arm, but in speech and action she was rarely available as a mother to a daughter. With those glazed worried eyes, she was often gone before she died.

Despite her imperceptible psyche, her emotional and psychological truancy, she didn't neglect us where matters of the physical were concerned. In that domain she had complete awareness of our health and carried the responsibility for our bodies close to her heart. She cooked all our meals. She was adamant that our shoes wouldn't pinch our lengthening toes. No shoe with a heel was allowed anywhere near my feet because she didn't want my arches to fall or my back squished into a crooked shape before I'd finished stretching into womanhood. When she saw that I'd scratched my back red raw because my skin was painfully dry and itchy we went to Boots to get cream to sooth it. That perfect No. 7 glass pot with its dark blue lid and silver label. For a couple of nights she rubbed it in, caressed my skin with the rich cool white cream. To have her touch, I triumphed under it. Her hands on me.

When I was a toddler, a pan of boiling water was accidentally knocked off the stove by a family friend. It poured over me and left me badly burnt. To stop my chest from scarring my mother kept me inside the house for several days to deter any infection. I ran around naked getting air to the burns and my skin healed perfectly because of her patience. She said it nearly drove her mad being cooped up like a chicken, but for her there was no choice, she would not have allowed me to carry the mark of the burns if she could prevent it.

She hated it when my body was scarred or damaged. When I landed on my face whilst playing in the school playground blood shot out of the bridge of my nose. My mother was called in to school to take me to the doctor, but decided it was unnecessary for me to see one, thinking I didn't need stitches. Half protective, half curious, Callum inspected the wound. He told me I'd hate it when I was older if there was a scar and that I shouldn't touch the scab because I'd make it worse. When a tiny dent of a scar did make its home on my face one inch from my eye, Mum asked me if I wanted to have it tidied up by a surgeon. This was unlike her, she wasn't particularly bothered about looks. I told her I really didn't care about it, when you're a child the comparison of scars is a time-consuming playground pastime of some importance. It never did come to annoy me, but she remained frustrated she hadn't taken me to have those stitches.

In her preoccupied mind she still had an awareness of the physical.

But where was she when she wasn't with us? Slowly bleeding dry, loving and leaving in all her moves. Words were what I wanted, from a mouth that seemed mercilessly inaudible. She was banished to quarters for the injured, the emotionally maimed. And because I didn't know of any life before Gareth, I didn't know if she had always been like that, or if she had become so as a result of the strains his state created.

When she and I moved away from home I was thirteen, I thought things would change because I'd have her to myself. Instead I became worried for her, for her newfound vulnerability. She looked bemused, a little suspicious of somewhere new and unknown. Life without Gareth was quiet. It was hard to know what to do with yourself, a new way of life would have to be carved out. Maybe better the devil you know.

We moved into a rented house with a long, long garden. The first section was well looked after, cut grass, an apple tree, pruned rose bushes, daisies and snowdrops. The second section was less tame, like a meadow free to grow but not yet wild. The grass was long, our feet disappeared in the green and slyly it tickled our bare legs. The third section was full of brambles, disorderly bushes of berries, protruding thorns. It was overcrowded, as if these plants couldn't grow enough, couldn't absorb enough carbon dioxide, they would never cease claiming space. You could get lost in it. In the fading sunlight I stood in the middle of that patch wondering what was going to happen to us now that we had left. I didn't know how the two of us would live together alone. Our new circumstances were calmer than what we were used to, but it felt to me as though we were on the run.

Before my new school started I spent my days with my mother. I cooked for her. I wanted to take care of this person who looked fragile, and because otherwise she wouldn't bother eating. She had never eaten much, the only food she had regularly consumed was the thickly buttered toast my father had made her every morning. For the first time I saw her clear plates of food. Maybe I wanted to build her up so that she could protect me. I bought her flowers and she was thrilled.

I had always wanted her to teach me how to draw and paint, and now it started to happen. We spread newspaper out on the dining room table and placed objects from the kitchen on it for me to draw with coloured charcoals. The dry colour rubbed into my fingers. It felt decadent to have the powdery dust of her on me. She took it seriously, and as she explained the principles of perspective to me I realized the resolve that she applied to her living. I was beginning to see her.

Then I began school and everything was awful. I was the new outsider, the new girl who was fair game. I missed my friends, I missed London, I missed what I knew. When I told her how unhappy I was she turned around in anger.

'I never asked you to come here,' she said, dizzy with a spite she had never thrown at me before. A split second later she claimed she didn't mean it but the cruel words were freed from her mouth, unable to climb back in. True, she hadn't asked me to come with her in so many words. She had said she was planning to leave home and that where she was moving to had a good school, and would I like to meet the headmaster? After I met him she showed me the house she planned to rent, highlighting the bedroom that could be mine if I chose to stay with her. In the weeks before she left she started buying me navy clothes, the designated colour of the school's uniform. Even as she drove me and my boxes of belongings to Oundle I had not agreed to live with her. The boundaries hadn't been marked.

She suggested that I return home and live with my father and Gareth. We called Dad up and he seemed reluctant. He hadn't bargained on having to look after his children alone. But he said yes, I could come home and live with him. I did, and visited my mother most weekends.

With the gradual admission of who Mum was to me, the way she was when she was around me, the more vexed and furious and guilty I become.

I had hidden her sadness in a bleak corner of my mind, put it in the basement so as not to sway my beliefs. That is not where I come from. I refuse to fall through the same crack as her though I see it all the same, a widening ravine, a sporadic threat. And I don't know why I have not yet turned into her. Sometimes I feel that I might earn her fate because she's not here to question and give me her dented armour.

Of course she did not fall. She was pushed.

I take the angel cloak away from my mother and she withdraws from me. I no longer feel her around. Before, she was there, around in the shadows, seeing what we were up to. I have felt more watched over in her death than during her life. She was drifting for a while, still a mother, spirit mother watching. Now she really has gone.

I go to her grave and for the first time in years the curling black wrought iron gates are locked. I must have known they would be as it is late in the evening, but I have waited until the sun clocked off and the barricading swirls which adorn the place bar me from her ashes. In the rain I prop up the drooping purple flowers I've brought for her against the gates. She has stopped me seeing her.

I take off her rings that I have worn for years. I want to be free of her now. As they slip off my fingers part of the twisting dwelling just below my breastbone siphons off. It releases with the speed that air is drawn into the lungs when emerging from a breath held beneath the water.

After she died I became overly attached to her engagement ring. As a child I had found it when rifling through her jewellery box. She was getting ready in the bathroom to go out with my father, I was hanging around vying for attention and observing her process of glamming up.

Our bathroom was an unattractive 1970s brown, brown tiles from floor to ceiling. My mother's jewellery box lived on one of the shelves of the rambling carved wooden foliage of her black mirror which covered nearly the whole wall. She was wearing a long black dress that hugged her body loosely. A magpie, I reached for the object that was glinting at me, but before I'd got it out the box she said, 'Be careful with that, it's worth quite a bit.'

'Is it your engagement ring?' I asked. She replied that it was and carried on brushing her hair, hurriedly trying to leave the house.

She never wore it and I didn't see it again until she was dead. When Callum and I went through her belongings we found it, still there in her jewellery box, along with her thin, gold wedding band. Her only daughter, it was mine without question. I put it on the fourth finger of my right hand, it fitted perfectly, we had the same size hands, and I didn't take it off for years.

I believed she was with me when I wore her ring, a maternal talisman. I had recurring dreams in which the stones fell out of it. I found them disturbing. Losing her again, having her fall away. I felt in some superstitious way that if the stones went, she would too. Unaware I was doing it, countless times a day I would stretch the pad of my thumb to the base of my fourth finger and press down to check that the three diamonds and the two sapphires were still there, sitting in the delicate gold winding setting which held them safe.

One evening, when I was with Sami in her flat, we had just finished eating supper and my thumb did the unthinking action it did several times a day. It reached and pressed, and to my horror I felt the hollow. My thumb scraped the thinning claws that had let the central diamond go. Their harshness without a stone, their unremitting scratchiness, how they were spiky around the empty space. I could barely speak to say what was wrong. I ran outside. Sami and her brother followed me into the street, we searched for it even though it was dark. Like idiots examining the ground. A tiny diamond, a needle in a haystack. I knew we wouldn't find it. I didn't know when I'd lost it, didn't know when I'd felt it last. Diamond in the gutter. Dad had the missing stone replaced for my eighteenth birthday.

Shortly after the diamond incident, I was walking down the street and saw an old friend coming from the opposite direction. When we met one another she told me that for a second she thought I was Mum, that for a second the awareness of her death had left her, and in the distance I had looked like my mother. She had been dead for a few years by then and it was consuming to think I might be mistaken for her. Did that mean I had come to resemble her since she died? A redundant question when I cannot look to compare. Briefly I felt pride in the thought that I might have. When you dress up in your mother's clothes as a child, there is some entrancing hope that one day you will be like her. I had, maybe, become like her after she had gone, even without her presence to absorb.

Another time, again a few years after her death, at a dinner party given by a friend of the family, a stranger came up to me and said, 'I was sorry to hear about your mother. You know you have your mother's eyes.'

I didn't know what to say. I didn't know whether or not I wanted to have them.

In my mid-twenties the skin at the tips and sides of my fingers started to crack. Deep, dry lines opened up which were rough to the touch. I remembered hers had been like that too, furrows that became filled with paint, greyness, trapped smudginess. I was growing my mother's fingers. My skin had recalled its heritage, the past before me, written in my flesh.

I wonder if you learn depression. If it isn't just about genes, like eyes and hands, but if you learn from watching. I panic over the extent to which we might form ourselves through imitation, that mental states are contagious.

The good doctors were right. She did suffer from depression.

The memories stop and I'm back, learning about my family from the notes.

Mum was desperate. She wrote a letter to Gareth's doctor on 17 June 1989.

I have to say I am prepared to do anything to help Gareth except live with him. The result would be a murder or a suicide pact. I realize that this sounds dramatic, but life with Gareth has been unbearably so.

She had already left our family home when she wrote this but was still heavily involved in the matter of what to do with Gareth. The enigma no one knew how to handle. She'd accepted by then there was no remedy, that it was a matter of how to cope. In this letter she arranged a meeting with two of Gareth's doctors. There was the issue of where he should be living, whether he should be institution-alized or left at home with Dad and myself, and what the consequences of either were likely to be.

I read the minutes from the talk, am taken back in time to past words said. She talks of me, even though she rarely talked *to* me about any of this.

She started off by saying that her main worry was about Gareth's sister Harriet who is fifteen. Mrs Gordon has been worried that Harriet has been Gareth's only support and putting considerable strain on her and indeed there has recently been a row between Gareth and Harriet and Harriet is now avoiding going home. Harriet is described as always being very protective towards Gareth especially when he came back from Northgate Clinic.

The row happened because I had had enough of watching my step, missing the dirt-filled lines between the paving stones or else. Doing and saying anything to keep the peace. For her, keeping the peace and survival were synonymous. For me, it was no longer tolerable to entertain his paranoia. If he couldn't handle everyday life around me then he shouldn't be around me. There was a cleft in my patience, cracked deep as soil in a drought. I wanted to exhale in what was supposed to be our home.

It was true that I had been protective, perhaps more accurately I had looked after him in certain ways. After she left home I shopped for him, bought his clothes and food, sometimes cooked for him and filled in forms for him, because he was unable or unwilling to do those things for himself. Some protection.

But something tore and I stopped balancing. It had gradually dawned on me that I couldn't be bound by him. I wanted to support him, but not at the expense of myself. I would not sacrifice myself in the way my mother had herself, and shortly before she died it became clear how much she had endured in trying to help him.

Heaving distortions reigned prolifically in his thoughts. I was trying to get inside his head. I was trying to control him. Then one day, following one of my mother's regular visits to him, with villainous rage, he shouted out that I was manipulating her. I went nuts. I'd lost her to him early on in life and he was accusing me. The gall, I couldn't stand it. For the first time I shouted back at him, I thought he was going to hit me and I wouldn't have cared if he had, I had stopped feeling the blows long ago. Surprisingly he didn't raise a finger. I ran out of the house to my mother who was beginning to drive away, back to her sanctuary away from us. I told her if she wanted to have her life back she should leave Gareth alone.

She ignored me for a couple of weeks, didn't answer the phone when I called her house in Oundle. I dialled the number like a maniac, like a stalker. Feeling like I might die if she didn't answer. Turning the dial that took so long to whiz back in anticipation of the next number. It rang and rang, she didn't have an answering machine. Each time I waited until the BT message kicked in to tell me I should hang up and try again later. I dialled until the pads of my fingers knew the number better than my head. Still there was no answer. I was used to her absence, but I couldn't cope with her avoiding me. When she did eventually pick up the phone I told her I no longer wanted to come to her house as I normally did on weekends. I was never in my mother's house again with her, the next time we spoke she was in hospital.

Gareth and I didn't speak for weeks, that row was the first time I had ever challenged him. Until then I'd kept quiet towards him as he ruled our universe with his moods, his ups and downs.

One of the reasons I was so incensed by his jibe at me was because in his longing and need for help Gareth could be highly manipulative, even with those who supported him. There were facets of his behaviour that could, it appeared, be turned on and off at will. He wanted to be seen in a certain way, he wanted to prove his charisma, humour and intellect to doctors, as though he had to demonstrate his worth to them. My mother felt he possessed a kind of magic, that he delivered a charm that impressed doctors and others, that on occasion he got busy fooling the people who needed to see the whole in order to treat him. A magician who got caught in his own tricks.

Met Mrs Gordon. She feels she has had enough and wants to distance herself from Gareth. She feels he has always been a strange child, with superstitious ideas and a strange ability to 'enchant' other people.

She never did manage to distance herself, not until she was in hospital. During one of my visits to her sick bed she revealed she had thought a lot about what I'd said, about seeing Gareth less. She had come to agree with me, and decided that when she came out of hospital things would be different, that she would make her life her own. She never came out.

But how do you distance yourself from a child with paranoia and depression, how can you not succumb when they are your own? A child who grows into a young man with as many troubles as he had when he looked like a blond-haired angel, chaotic hair spilling onto his face. This child of the 70s. He wore ripped, blue, drainpipe jeans with a patch on the knee, his t-shirts had faded, the logos had gradually fallen off in the washing machine.

On Wednesday mornings my mother took our dirty clothes to the laundrette round the corner from our house. Then she'd go to the Sainbury's in Kentish Town, and the fruit and veg market in Inverness Street, Camden Town, before returning to pick the washing up. If one of us was ill and had the day off school we would accompany her on this outing. I loved it. When I went with her she would buy me an almond tart from the bakery. Its crusted pastry melted in my mouth, with the thin layer of jam which I wanted more of but knew would have been too sweet if there had been. The *pièce de résistance* was in the fine smattering of browned almonds that lay on top like a beach crammed with sunbathing bodies.

In the market it surprised me that she always knew exactly what to buy from the fruit and veg stalls that tantalized you with colour neatly stacked in crates, so carefully placed that if the wrong orange were removed everything might tumble down and roll across the pavement. When she asked for a pound of apples, or two of onions, her efficiency bemused me. How did she know how many apples were in a pound? In my infant head I quantified adulthood, you must reach it when you know how many apples are in a pound. Not to mention being strong enough to tighten a hot-water bottle lid, secure in the knowledge that you are safely protected from the boiled water that might otherwise leak out in the night. Or when you're capable of stepping off escalators on your own. When I was small, as the top of the London under-ground escalator neared I would look up and grab my mother or father's hand to be deftly lifted up. Otherwise I might be eaten up by it, I thought, get caught in its teeth as it disappeared back into the ground.

Gareth's complications grew as he did. Accumulated as his cells divided. The difficult child became the difficult adult and it became apparent he wasn't going to grow out of his problems. And he became strong as he got older so the fear of him becoming angry was legitimate.

From as far back as I can remember, until I was about twelve, Gareth had hated me with a passion. The slightest thing could set him off. Looking at him in the wrong way, getting a larger portion of food than him at dinner, sitting in a chair that he wanted to sit in, or being in a room that he wanted to occupy alone. At breakfast we would sit on opposite sides of the table and my mother would put a cereal box between the two of us because if I looked at him he would hit me. If she caught him he would defensively attest, 'I only tapped her,' and he thought it so. I read the ingredients of our cereals one hundred times or more and repeatedly examined the tokens you needed to collect for a free gift. Keep so many tokens and the milkman will give you a Rice Krispies bowl. If I accidentally caught his eye he'd thump me. He couldn't stand the sight of me, so I did my best to disappear. And when I didn't there was trouble.

One incident began when I was on the phone to a school friend. We had been chatting a while when there was a click, the click of someone picking up the phone. Juliet and I waited for them to replace it, as anyone would when they heard that someone else was already on the line. They didn't. Juliet said there was no one else in her house. For a moment, having gorged on horror films every Friday night, we both went silent and knew we were thinking the same thing, an intruder must be in her house. Then we returned to reality and deduced that it must have been Gareth as he was the only person in our house. Feeling courageous because I had an ally I shouted down the stairs to ask Gareth to put the phone down. He did one of his flying manoeuvres. One minute he had been downstairs, the next he was upstairs and had brought my head down to the floor by my hair, a fine tool with which to drag my head. He shouted as I lay there unable to see through my hair over my eyes. One of his hands was pulling my head up by my hair and the other was pressing my head to the floor so that my neck was crunched back. He loomed above me as words came out his mouth for battle. How dare I speak to him like that. Who the fuck did I think I was? I had screamed as he brought my head to the floor.

Juliet was silent on the other end of the phone, but Gareth suddenly remembered her presence. Loudly he spoke, 'And don't you fucking dare tell her that I've hurt you. Because I haven't.' He started crying, saying that I was lying if I said anything because he hadn't touched me. When he let me go and I spoke with her, Juliet told me she'd heard the bang of my head on the floor.

When Gareth broke down he was more desperate than anyone I've ever seen. Confusion ran through his body like blood and water does through others. A violence shook through his expressions, extinguished any reason on his face. His eyes became rabid and empty all at once. His despairing wailing cries. The hurt at being hurt, the indignant pain that had the nerve to stride across him, engulfed him to his core.

He couldn't be rational, and in dealing with him on a daily basis we never knew how he would react. But after the ruckus he could be funny and warm and charming, and I felt ashamed for housing anger towards this great big gentle man. Though he spent all that time in psychiatric care I never thought of him as being mentally ill. I would have resented his imposing anarchy less if I'd realized he was, and though it sounds absurd I didn't when he was alive.

He certainly didn't believe he was mentally ill; it was the world against him, not his thoughts. By the time he was an adult, it was about his flesh, a swindle of transference, mental into physical pain. The shrieks in him became bodily wounds. Caged in a host ruled by the mind.

Things would get broken, furniture, glasses, crockery and banisters. Sometimes he would lash out at one of us, and he would do so quickly.

Once he came at me because I called him Scrumple. It was the nickname Callum had given him, though used only when he wasn't in earshot. Gareth hated it even though it was intended as a term of endearment. My mother said if she'd heard it before Gareth was born she might have named him Scrumple because it was such a wonderfully round word. Just once I used it to his face. I hadn't meant to, it slipped out without me thinking. He was in the garden and I said the 'S' word to him from my bedroom window. Within seconds he had left the garden, ascended two flights of stairs and was in my bedroom doorway just as I was trying to escape. My mother too had flown because she knew what he might do to me. She attempted to get between he and I as he flung his fists around. His face came up close to mine and he tried to hit me but barely succeeded because she had managed to fill the gap between us. This scramble lasted for several minutes until she somehow got him to withdraw.

He could turn in an instant. You could be having a laugh with him one minute and the next he'd have you pinned down to the floor. And he could zoom up or down the stairs with such speed that I didn't have a chance to get away. As if he had wings, he flew to your face to fight it.

My fear was his speed, his reactions were instantaneous. That was the difficulty in living with him, you never knew when he would blow and you never knew if he would do damage.

Gareth wasn't violent in the sense that he'd beat you up. He wouldn't have you in a heap on the floor and hit you black and blue until you couldn't move, which was what I thought violence was. He didn't do that, nor did he pull and pinch as siblings do. What he did, was get you when he felt you'd got him. He dealt blows that bruised. I never made the link with violence. Gareth's behaviour was normal to me.

In the bath I used to look at the bruises on my legs and arms, their multiple blue hues. They had been there for as long as I could remember so I didn't question where they had come from. They were in fact a part of me, because they were incessant. Bruises on skin, the purple mottled surface which remembers the thwack for longer than the psyche. It's hard, if not impossible, to memorize the sensation of physical pain beyond its impact, but bruises, bruises show the strike. They testify to the moving fist, to the force behind the thump, to the anger it was invested with, to the shoe hurled at your tibia, to the smack of inert skin against the tightness of a raw clenched fist. As clean as brakes on a brand new car. Willows of reddish purple veins making streams off the centrepiece, spreading to increase its territory on your skin. When Gareth went to boarding school they became fewer, nearly disappeared. Then one weekend when he came home, a friend of ours who Gareth was very fond of, told him if he didn't stop thumping me completely she would never speak to him again. After that, he only touched me a couple more times. Years later when Callum asked him why he used to hit me, he innocently denied all knowledge of ever having done so, and I questioned the purple composites' past existence.

Soon after he stopped my mother admitted she had been scared he was going to cause permanent damage.

I responded with surprise, it never having occurred to me that he could have.

'Really?'

'Yes.'

'Was it that bad?' I asked, curiously truncated from my body.

'Yes,' she said, louder, annoyed and with more force, because I hadn't understood what was apparently obvious. It left me confused. If she thought it was that bad then why didn't she stop it?

When she told me, because I didn't remember, that he had tied me to the lamp post in the street when I was tiny and left me there

while he went into the house for dinner, and that it was the neighbours who had come out and untied me, all I could think about was
why it wasn't she who had let me loose. I couldn't get to grips with
her not dealing with things that happened.

I get Gareth's notes from the Northgate Clinic, where he'd
stayed for a while when he was eighteen. When I thank the psychol-
ogist who treated my brother for them he says resolutely, 'It is your
right.' My right to have more history. In them is a letter Mum had
written to a doctor after Gareth was taken into hospital following
an overdose. It was penned late at night out of desperation to try
and get them to understand what it had been like from her
perspective.

After two days the hospital told me that I could take Gareth home.
I said I couldn't and that he needed treatment or he would be back
in no time. 'Where can he go?' said his sister and that was that. They
gave me four more days. Gareth came back and the nightmare
continued. Not waking, not eating, not sleeping until the night was
almost over. No hope, nothing to do except beat up his sister and
watch telly. His treatment of his sister appalled me. I used to have to
put a huge box of cereal between them in case Hattie looked at
Gareth. If their eyes met she got beaten. If they passed on the stairs she
got beaten. The unhappier that Gareth became the harder he hit her.
It was difficult to be angry with someone in such a mess but of course
I had to show that I disapproved of his behaviour. When I showed
this disapproval he hit Hattie. I feared for her fertility. It was
impossible to keep them apart all the time and anyway I shouldn't
have to.

Then I understood, it was like everything else. There was no way
of stopping him and even attempting to do so made things worse.

I do remember trying to resist the urge to look at him. Fighting
with my eyes not to rise. I was inquisitive though, if I looked would

he catch me doing so? What if I gained a glimpse of him without him seeing, would that somehow mean I had beaten him at his own game? It was a futile riddle, but the urge to look when you know you can't, that was hard to overcome. Almost, I wanted to see the glare in his eye for more than a split second before the thud. What was in there that wanted to hit me? What was in my eyes that made him want to attack? Would he be able to hold a look with me before the punch? If he looked would he then not be able to?

On the stairs I would sink into the wall. Flatten my reed-thin self against it, giving him all the space and praying he might not notice me because I had squashed myself as much as I could. Into the funny wallpaper that looked as though rice had been scattered behind it. I turned my face to the wall and looked down so I couldn't be accused of catching his eye, of challenging him and his eyes that didn't want to see me. The one who was supposed to be unseen, so why was I on the stairs? I couldn't explain why I was there because I shouldn't have been. He saw and he punched. What I could do though, if there was time, if I heard him coming but couldn't yet see him, was run. Flee, up the stairs, quickly, as if I'd never been there. And I was fast because my legs were long and supple, they served me well. At school I was the fastest sprinter. That was more effective than trying to be invisible because he rarely came after me, he just got me if I was there.

My mother had her own encounters with his strength. Just as she had wrestled with Gareth to stop him jumping out of the car, she fought with him to stop him cutting himself with a knife. I remember her mentioning the knife fight in passing, and then I read about it in her letter within the clinic's notes. Her leaning writing telling me more.

Once we had a struggle with a very sharp kitchen knife and smashed a cupboard door. I got blood poisoning. My arm swelled to amazing propor-

tions and I had to take to my bed. Gareth looked after me and brought me drinks. Unfortunately penicillin repaired me and in no time I was up and about again and grappling with the madhouse.

I read, too, about that first liaison with pills, discovered how it unfolded.

When I went up to see him he seemed sleepier than usual and the puppy was licking him all over in a desperate effort at waking him. I started to shake him awake as usual. It was a process that always took ages, but I was a little suspicious. I couldn't wake him and went back to getting the meat chopped up for the family supper. Shortly afterwards I heard him being violently sick. I went up to him and felt sure he had taken an overdose. He had been threatening for a long time but I didn't believe he would ever do it. I asked him if he had eaten aspirins and he denied it. I asked him if he would come to the hospital with me but he refused. Although he was weakened by weeks in bed he was still strong from BMXing and I hadn't a hope of forcing him to come with me.

I went downstairs and finished preparing the supper. I could hear Gareth being sick again. I phoned 999. When the ambulance men came they asked Gareth why he had done it. He said, 'Everything went wrong.' . . . I have to say that with Gareth out of the house, I looked forwards to a night's sleep.

When he wasn't in hospital, there was little or no care for him. We were supposed to handle him, but we didn't know how to and no professional gave us advice on what was best for him, and us, when he was at home.

My feelings towards Gareth changed when my mother made the flippant comment that he disliked me because I was the apple of our father's eye and he was jealous. Like most things she spat it out as though it were common knowledge.

'You know he's envious of you because of Dad.'

From then on I decided that I would make a concerted effort to be nice to him rather than just keep out of his way. I wrote him letters while he was at boarding school, one a week, so that he would receive something before he came home for the weekend. I started buying him small gifts for when he arrived on a Friday night, peace offerings. I made fudge and cakes for him so that he would feel spoilt by food.

Our time was invested with caution on my part – aggression and vulnerability in the same person was difficult to deal with. You couldn't just say anything, you couldn't rock his imbalance. That fine, intricate blend of depression and whatever else it was he possessed, which if teetered, if upheaved, unleashed itself. I would try and say all the right things to make him feel better, but didn't know if I might accidentally suggest or do something to make him flip. It was a tightrope walk, an act that could easily, and often did, go wrong. But we became fond of one another, we began to laugh together and enjoy each other's company.

Later, while I was living with my father and Gareth was a resident at the Northgate Clinic, he became very protective of me. He didn't like leaving me alone in the house and went through a phase of visiting me in the evening and not leaving until Dad had come home. It served us both well, Gareth was under the illusion that he was taking care of me, and I that I was taking care of him. I would cook him dinner, so at the very least I could persuade myself that he was getting nourishment. It also meant I knew where he was. If he was with me, he wasn't trying to do himself in. He stayed around and acted as a protective body, against what I was never sure. He just didn't want me to be left alone. Maybe it was because his own loneliness tore him to shreds on a daily basis.

Though it seems like there weren't, there were many times when he smiled. I miss Gareth's sense of humour. The strangest things would fascinate him and make him laugh. That infectious laughter, one which makes your sides ache, your body reeling with the vibration passing through. Indicative of his particular strain of humour was that Gareth delighted in the fact that someone once died of a heart attack brought on by laughing too hard at a *Carry On* film.

He laughed a lot with one of our babysitters. Gareth loved him because he let us get up to all sorts. We used to load hot chocolate powder onto spoons and run around blowing it over each other. Clouds of brown dust would hang in the air as we scampered around the house getting coated in chocolate. Gareth's hoots of laughter billowed out from the chocolate dust. It was Sean who gave us our first drag on a cigarette – he did it to demonstrate what a foul habit smoking is. Eagerly we pursed the white stick as inelegantly as any child smoker, then had the mandatory coughing fit afterwards.

While on a family holiday on the Spanish island of Formentera, when I was in my early teens, Gareth and I shared an apartment. He was lying on his stomach on the tiled veranda floor enjoying the sun on his back. His chin was propped up on his hands so that he could watch the world that wasn't having a siesta go by.

Our apartment had attracted a lot of cats, several litters had been born nearby. He watched them run to their mothers, puny things, wobbling on their dainty legs, unable yet to stride with feline regality. Geckos darted across the white walls above him before losing their transient tails. Flicking around as though they'd touched something burning hot.

As I walked in front of him he started rolling around. He couldn't speak for his howling laughter.

'What's so funny?' I asked, fully aware that he had only started laughing as I had moved. Did I have something stuck to my face or hair or what? Finally he drawled, 'It's your feet.'

'My what?'

'Your feet.'

'Have you gone mad?'

'Feet are so funny when they move,' and he continued to laugh. He asked me to walk back and forth in front of him so that he could look and laugh at my feet. I padded the scorching tiles like the geckos. He then volunteered to walk in front of me if I lay on the ground and watched his feet. Later, his hysteria made me look at other people's feet. One man's eccentricity is another man's madness.

Feet.

Gareth, a year before he died

Chapter Nine

Throughout the years of coping with Gareth, my mother wasn't helped by the authorities, by the people she should have been helped by. On sheet after sheet of paper, it is clear she had been dying of despair. I see in a letter that at one point she did get some support. She mentions someone, Sarah Allen, a social worker who had worked with my mother and Gareth and understood the 'family situation'. She wrote that Sarah had known what she'd been through. *I think Sarah Allen at the Tavistock Clinic understands my position. She helped me drag myself through five years of horrendous family life.* I call Sarah, maybe she can tell me something about Mum that will make her less obscure to me. I assume that she won't want to talk to me, it was years ago after all, she might not even remember us. I get through to her and she is prepared to speak with me but says she's not sure what I want.

'I want your memory.'

She says she would like to meet me.

I want to see her for answers. I hope for something that will make me feel like I knew my mother, so she won't be the figure in the shadows. I've had only glimpses of her, and these don't make up the whole. Even though the missing parts are gone, still I want someone to tell me where they were when she was here.

I go to the clinic where my mother and Gareth went. Sarah fetches me from the waiting room. 'You must be Hattie.'

We sit in her office and she tells me her memories of my mother. She says she was very fond of her, and recalls she had a great sense of humour. She had spoken with her regularly for about two years, my mother used to come and see her after her daily morning swim. She says there really isn't anything to tell me that will help, like everyone else she affirms Mum was a very private person. Those words in my ears like a mantra working hard to keep her from me. Perhaps it's best if I don't know certain things, she tells me. I don't give a damn about her privacy, I want her. I say I can deal with anything, what I can't deal with is not knowing. She says there are things she shouldn't tell me because it would be unfair to my mother. It would be unfair to me, I think, she's dead and I'm alive.

With a smile she tells me my mother was fey. Sarah likes that she was. Fey. Distracted to the point of being somewhere else. Majestically she walked through forests, perhaps with fairies. Fey looks away, askew. And when she looks back her eyes would be somewhere else. Fey cannot be chased. Fey could be marvellous and eccentric, could reveal other worlds. Lose yourself from this one. But that's not how I saw her. Maybe fey was how she started, disappear was what she did.

It was a long time ago, she'll have a think and if anything comes back she'll contact me.

Towards the end of our meeting she says, 'She was desperately worried about the effect everything was having on you. You know your mother did the very best she could under the circumstances. You should remember that. She coped as best she could. And she thought you were very sensible. She thought you coped very well.'

I tell her that's absurd, a child is a child and shouldn't be expected to cope. 'She did the best she could.'

'Did she ever say she wanted to kill herself?' I ask, and the words burn my tongue and lips as they are formed. I'm scorched under the weight of them. Is this the thing that kept her hidden from me, kept her away, was it a suicidal depression or just the standard stuff? Does it run in the family, a rogue gene, the mark waiting to appear?

'No, she never said that to me.' Relief. If she didn't want to die then she couldn't have wanted to leave us.

'But she found the demands between working and being a mother difficult. She definitely had a refuge in her work. She really enjoyed it and I felt that it was often what kept her going.'

Next I go through a file of notes from another clinic Gareth attended. In it I find letters both from my mother and about her, including a letter from Sarah.

'We were also concerned for Mrs Gordon. She was extremely depressed and confused, and frightened both of Gareth and of her own suicidal thoughts. She would become quite incoherent and rambling in her confusion.'

I read it many times.

Did she forget, or does she think she needs to protect me? The family in 'very serious trouble'. Does she think I'm at risk of the mind thieves too? I'd told her I'd rather know than not, that the confusion was more unbearable than the tragedy. Maybe she decided I was wrong, that I didn't know my own mind. I feel pushed and pulled.

In the same letter my mother's and Gareth's relationship is described as a *folie à deux*, a condition first described and given its name in 1887. A double insanity, also known as shared paranoid disorder, induced psychotic disorder, contagious insanity, infectious insanity and communicated insanity. With this *folie* it is believed that two closely associated people experience a psychosis simultaneously, and that one of the pair has influenced the other. Sometimes more than two people are involved, entire families have been known to suffer from it. The person in the dominant position is usually schizophrenic or affected by a similar psychotic disorder. In this case, Mum would have influenced Gareth. So was she deluded and Gareth shared in the delusions? Would his illness not have existed without her psychotic mind?

They've made my mother monstrous. According to them the problem didn't originate with Gareth. It wasn't that my mother couldn't cope with a difficult and then suicidal son, it was that she had instilled illness in him, that she had singled him out as different from the moment she was pregnant with him and therefore instigated it. She didn't have a hard pregnancy, she'd imagined it.

It is written too that she was referred for psychotherapy, but after one session they had decided not to treat her.

I make a formal request to see the notes from the clinic where my mother used to go and see Sarah. I want the rest of what they know. It is my right, I remember. On hearing nothing I call to find out how long it will take to process.

'I'm very sorry but we can't find the file.'

'You mean you've lost it?'

'Well, we're still looking for it.'

They've lost my paper brother and mother.

'What will you do if you can't find the notes?'

'We normally come to some arrangement.'

'You mean people normally accept that they are lost?'

'Look, we're not infallible you know. Even if we find them we don't have to show them to you.'

I'm supposed to accept this like a good little girl.

Days later they call to tell me they've found them. They ask for my father's permission for me to see the notes and he immediately gives it.

I go back to the clinic to pick up the papers and see Sarah again. I still want her memory. I ask her about the *folie à deux*. She says perhaps they shouldn't have used that term, it was a long time ago.

'We merely meant that they were enmeshed.'

I ask why my mother was referred for psychotherapy. The answer is frank.

'There was some question as to how Gareth got hold of the aspirin.'

Did she too think death would stop the pain? Did she give him the idea, is that how he learnt it? Is that why she didn't call the ambulance straight away? Is that why she kept on cooking? Must feed the family even if he's dying upstairs? Did she want the pills to kick in before they got there? How desperate can a mother get?

I read the notes written when Gareth was barely a teenager. Following his first overdose, the typed words say that the doctors at the Royal Free Hospital ... *realized Mrs Gordon had given him the aspirin he used for the overdose, and also gave him razor blades. But that he had seemed so cheerful in hospital they had under-estimated the disturbing nature of the information, and also the severity of Gareth's disturbance.*

Underestimated that her hands gave him the weapon.

She was in danger of killing him. She was a potential criminal.

'Why wasn't she seen then?'

'She was too fragmented to undergo psychotherapy. It was a matter of holding her together, not one of taking her apart.'

Tucked away in the file is a handwritten letter by Mum.

The grisly ordeal just kept on and on. I found if I drank a fair amount at least it numbed the pain a little. I didn't know what to do. No one helped. No one advised. I couldn't eat and Gareth gave me no chance to sleep. I started to have fantasies about killing him. I thought that if I could somehow get him to drink a bottle of whiskey I could quickly hit him over the head with the mallet we used for banging in the pegs when we went camping.

I understood my mother once I'd read it, read her own words of desperation. I got her confusion, the chaos of her mind, the not knowing if her life would ever be liveable without being held captive to her son. Why she wasn't there. Why her psyche never found mine. The drink in the bedroom. The coldness and the static grey eyes. The impossibility of stopping Gareth's violence. The giving up on daily life. The happiness at being laid up in hospital. The facts that fitted neatly into the atmosphere at home. And I got why she was ready to die. 'One Day I'll Fly Away.' She was carried far, to where she needed to be. She needed to abscond. I hear the sound of her leaving, the waves of her hair as they fall upon her shoulders.

In the three sets of notes I have, doctors, psychiatrists and specialists continued to make their summaries about Gareth. Mostly they reiterate the last person's observations and rarely express anything new. Occasionally leaps are made beyond depression, but they don't seem to be followed through. Will going over the facts, the same facts, help?

March 1984 – *I have no doubt that the picture is complex and Gareth is a child in considerable emotional difficulties.*

August 1988 – *He struck me as being a very depressed and troubled boy with some paranoid ingredients in the picture.*

April 1989 – *Gareth has had an extremely disturbed background ... It seems as though part of the problem is that Gareth as a* consequence of his long-term institutionalization has very little in the way of social skills or coping skills.

May 1989 – *As you know, Gareth is an eighteen-year-old man with very long-standing problems. Since childhood he has suffered from severe episodes of severe depression on the basis of a depressive personality. Often predominant are preoccupations with physical health, particularly pain behind the eyes (which has been extensively investigated), I believe that the possibility of myalgic encephalomyelitis is currently being investigated.*

August 1989 – *I discussed our tentative diagnosis [with my mother] – depression in the background of a schizoid personality disorder. (I explained that this was nothing to do with schizophrenia and that it would be difficult to know how much progress could be made with him until we have a better idea of how much is personality.)*

February 1990 – He has a long history of mood disturbance and enormous psychosocial difficulties going as far back as childhood. At the moment, in my opinion, he suffers from profound endogenous depression, exacerbated by his mother's death on New Year's Eve.

May 1990 – *I think ultimately he will turn out to have a form of post-viral fatigue syndrome which happens to have affected an individual who is previously very disturbed psychologically.*

April 1993 – *He was reviewed by a number of specialists including Professor ⸺ who felt that Aspergers syndrome though possible was not probable.*

In July 1994, just months before his death, the diagnosis on a discharge report at the end of a section was *Psychotic depression with somatic delusions.*

The rollercoaster had run out of control for years.

In the report about his 'Past Psychiatric History' following his death in early September 1994, the diagnosis is *Depression, Somatization*

Disorder, Personality Disorder; Borderline type. I look these up in the World Health Organization's *Classification of Mental and Behavioural Disorders*, the standard text used in psychiatry.

I read:

Somatization Disorder.

The main features are multiple, recurrent, and frequently changing physical symptoms, which have usually been present for several years before the patient is referred to a psychiatrist. Most patients have a long and complicated history of contact with both primary and secondary medical services, during which many negative investigations or fruitless operations may have been carried out. Symptoms may be referred to any part or system of the body, but gastrointestinal sensations (pain, belching, regurgitation, vomiting, nausea, etc.), and abnormal skin sensations (itching, burning, tingling, numbness, soreness, etc.) and blotchiness are among the commonest. Sexual and menstrual complaints are also common.

Marked depression and anxiety are frequently present and may justify specific treatment.

The course of the disorder is chronic and fluctuating, and is often associated with long-standing disruption of social, interpersonal, and family behaviour. The disorder is far more common in women than in men, and usually starts in early adult life.

Dependence upon or abuse of medication (usually sedatives and analgesics) often results from frequent courses of medication.

Diagnostic guidelines

A definite diagnosis requires the presence of all of the following:

a) at least 2 years of multiple and variable physical symptoms for which no adequate physical explanation has been found;

b) persistent refusal to accept the advice or reassurance of several doctors that there is no physical explanation for the symptoms;

c) some degree of impairment of social and family functioning attributable to the nature of the symptoms and resulting behaviour.

Borderline type.

Several of the characteristics of emotional instability are present; in addition, the patient's own self-image, aims, and internal preferences (including sexual) are often unclear or disturbed. There are usually chronic feelings of emptiness. A liability to become involved in intense and unstable relationships may cause repeated emotional crises and may be associated with excessive efforts to avoid abandonment and a series of suicidal threats or acts of self-harm (although these may occur without obvious precipitants).

When I have finished going through the notes, one of Gareth's psychiatrists tells me that had he lived, more could be done for him today. There are hundreds of anti-depressants nowadays, he'd have more of a chance than with the self-righteous fickle pills. They could try different combinations, start again with the medication. See if his body and mind and brain could be manipulated after all.

When my heart is pulled in the night, I wonder who is pulling it. Is it them, the unreachable reaching? They wrench me, hard, from my sleep. Dead immortal souls. When you die you lose the privilege of touch. Lose the senses that guided you through living. Tears are the only physical presence they have left. Yet they constantly touch me, tracing with fingertips that are curious and seek. I feel the stroke of another passing over me even as I'm alone. The touch is barely there, it makes me wonder if I really perceived it. Fair hairs stand on end as skin motions under an invisible pressure. Hands stretch from walls, to be drawn back into this time.

My body turns cold. Cold as water in the deepest part of the river, the part which draws back the dirt on the bottom as it passes through. Dank. Let me feel their breath just once. See the heat they owned as it leaves their mouths.

They exert an influence, the dead over the living. Memories run through my blood, blood remembers and it calls. Never does it clot, or dry with a beauty which would allow rest.

I decide to call a doctor Gareth had been involved with for several years before he died. This Harley Street man had developed a unique allergy treatment and felt that my brother was an ideal candidate for it. He thought that everything that was wrong with Gareth had a physical basis. He wrote that any psychiatrist who thought he could cure Gareth's depression without treating the physical underlying condition was deluding himself.

After Gareth had his first meeting with him, he proudly informed us that this doctor was convinced he would feel completely different in three years time if he underwent his specialist regime. He knew what was wrong with him, and he could explain it as no one else had done, and he could help, Gareth said. What a feat that would have been, to be the doctor that made him well.

Gareth became incredibly fond of him. Often he would go to his office just to have a chat. The feelings were reciprocated.

The course of treatment involved an extremely precise elimination diet and regular injections to re-train the body's responses to allergens. The theory was he was allergic to practically everything, which was why, Gareth explained to me, he always felt stoned without even touching recreational drugs.

While in hospital, Gareth would prepare his food in the kitchen, boiling specified combinations of meat and vegetables until they became a thick pulp. It was as if he was regressing to infantile ways of eating. He prepared these concoctions religiously, buying the right root vegetables, chopping them up, turning them into unappetising mush, and dutifully ingesting it. Lamb and yams became his staples, he and I would go to the local market and buy the strangest looking yams we could find. The odder the shape the better as far as he was concerned. They became forms to be reckoned with, this one had more sticky out bits than that one, but that one had an odder shape.

When Gareth was born his hair had been white blonde. As he got older it turned into a streaky honey blonde. As this diet progressed his hair turned from blonde to brown. It got duller as the diet went on, until it had lost all its colour and taken on a grey mousy appearance. His skin became sallow. He lost a tremendous amount of weight. He went from being tall and thin to, it seemed, even taller and skinny. His cheeks began to hollow, became concave where before there were pockets of flesh beneath his high cheekbones. And the fitness and strength that had been so important to him wasted away as he did.

He came to believe that he shouldn't use toothpaste, as he would be allergic to its ingredients. His teeth turned yellow. Our mother would have been appalled.

When we were children, once a year she put us through the ordeal of having fluoride treatment so that our teeth would remain lifelong strong. A foul tasting gel was squeezed into pink plastic moulds which were then stuck around our teeth for several minutes. Each year our dentist would tell us that there were new flavours: chocolate, strawberry or spearmint, attempting to endear us to what we considered a form of torture. But always they would taste as vile as the last time. We would sit in his chair counting the seconds of each minute, wishing the experience over as quickly as possible and trying not to gag.

Our teeth were strong thanks to Mum's insistence, until the yam diet.

Gareth had ups and downs on this program, as he had on every other treatment he'd undergone in his life. After one of the intermittent injections he deteriorated drastically. The doctor wrote: *Gareth became extremely disturbed and quite literally out of touch. He could not bear any form of human contact. He remained like this for several months.*

He said it might take another three years to cure him. Gareth was devastated. He had put all his hopes on this working, and started to lose that faith. Following an overdose, he was re-admitted to the Royal Free.

It then transpired he'd misunderstood much of the treatment and had been doing the diet all wrong, which would have hindered the whole process. He hadn't got the combinations of food right and he hadn't been preparing them as instructed. It posed the question of whether it was good judgement to put someone like Gareth on such a program, someone who found it hard to follow instructions, even if they were potentially beneficial to him. No doubt the process worked for some, but it hadn't for Gareth.

I call the doctor's office and leave a message on his answering machine. He doesn't return my call. I ring back several times and eventually speak to his secretary. She says if I phone at nine o'clock the following morning the doctor will speak to me then. When I do I am informed that he is too busy. When I ask her if he is avoiding talking to me she becomes defensive. 'To call up like this,' she pauses, 'after all this time.' The emphasis is on time, the word is drawn out like an uptight version of a Texan drawl. Was that the deal, had I left it too late to make enquiries about my brother? Is there is a limited amount of time to be curious? I wonder what she knows about time, about losing time to death.

After badgering her, he calls me that evening. He barely allows me to speak. He rattles off a monologue, telling me that Gareth's ills stemmed from his body. I ask him if he had thought about the complexities of treating a psychiatric patient for physical ailments. He reiterates that Gareth's psychological problems came from his body. The doctor doesn't address the fact that my brother came to believe he didn't require psychotherapeutic help because of his newfound conviction that all that was wrong lay in his flesh.

Gareth had started seeing a psychoanalyst at the Royal Free whilst seeing his Harley Street doctor. The analyst had to fight with the physical. He wrote:

I think that Mr Gordon may be amenable to a psychotherapy approach though I believe that it won't be an easy journey, especially because of his passive giving in to the 'organic component' to which he seems to latch on in order to confirm his long-standing dislike for his body and mind.

Soon after:

If Gareth can begin to recognize the large psychological component there is some hope for improvement.

The conclusion:

It became clear that his erratic attendance was an indication that he could not cope any longer with any form of psychotherapy and indeed part of him believed that it would not help anyway because of his deep conviction that his condition was of physical origin.

The Doctor ended his monologue by saying Gareth felt that 'life was just too shitty'. I think he's a quack with a brass nameplate. But I weep as I put the phone down.

Towards the end of his life Gareth became more and more aware of how institutionalized he had become over the years. He bore a sense of dread over the past which outweighed any optimism he might have conjured up for his future. As his depression left him in ways ever so slight, this became a reason in itself to be melancholic. He mourned for the life he'd missed. He lacked education, work experience and relationships he had faith in. He saw only what he didn't have, not what he could have. The stronger Gareth became the more he talked of what he'd missed out on. There seemed to be no going forward in thoughts or actions. He didn't know how to, didn't know how to move. Looking at the aftermath was too painful to live with. Like irredeemable previous actions one wants to erase but can't. Snatch the future before it replicates the past.

Chapter Ten

No one person's sense of history is the truth. No one person's sense of history is the untruth. Sometimes the laughter, precious laughter, makes me question the disturbed parts of his head, and they in turn make me question his laughter. Which is Gareth's truth? Both, but both confuse. I want things to be ordered and folded away so that I know – know who he could have been if he wasn't in his hell. Random fantasy. He was who he was. Never without the mangled mind. He grew into a head that turned against itself.

Others search for the bodies of their dead. Unable to rest until the body is buried. I know where their bodies went. I search for their souls instead.

I want to solve a history so that it might come to make more sense. That's why I looked at the notes, and there I found cold observation. Nothing that tells me why. I wanted to be told things that explained it all away. But nothing does. No one does. And I miss him, miss his cheeky face. Maybe all there is to know is that we lost Gareth, lost him to his mind. I cannot put the pieces together because their voices have gone. Silence in the wilderness. Their speaking fire put out when their hearts stopped beating. They died and so I cannot know their story. If we'd had just a few more years. But no. I want the dead to speak to me. Come to me and tell me.

They don't come to me after all my begging. Implored they were, but they don't come.

Easy to lose the living over the dead. I stop looking for them, and I look at what they left.

I look at me. I stare out of the window to the sea below the sunset. The sun going down seems like some terrible betrayal.

I recall my mother telling me once, 'Hattie, I found life very difficult in my late teens and early twenties.'

She said it as if it were a warning.

This comment of hers haunts me, because I, too, find life difficult sometimes. And at my lowest ebb I realize he'd been at least 100 times lower. His open wounds rubbed with salt, raw, without salve and bandages. I finally agree to take anti-depressants, having refused them for months after my doctor suggested they might be good for me. I convince myself that I am following in my mother and brother's genetic footsteps. I am reluctant to take the pills because I think it is the road to their endings. I don't want to live like my mother, when she was in bed with a bottle of wine and the silver packet of pills were shoved behind her scarves on the shelf in her wardrobe. Spots on leopards jeopardize any chance of change. The darkness may fall again, on me. I discuss my reservations with a wise nurse for nearly an hour. I realize I am privileged to get this time in the decimated climate of today's NHS.

I feel I have failed because I've got to the point where I have to take them or disintegrate further, remain paralysed and stagnate. I've been scared to swallow a single aspirin, let alone prescribed hits of serotonin.

I am one of the lucky ones, I have a good GP. Aged nineteen, when I had shingles on my back I kept them hidden as I thought my mother's illness had found its way to me because the sores looked the same. But my doctor differentiated her fatal illness and my sores. She took out her big fat book of afflictions, fanned through the hundreds of pages and looked up my mother's disease to assure me the two were unrelated.

Now she explains that my natural disposition affects what drugs I should take. If I'm anxious and shaky, she'll prescribe something that will calm me. If I'm stagnant, she'll give me something to pick me up. I think I am somewhere in-between, and that, she says, is fine.

Having been told they will take a few weeks to kick in, I take the first pill. I feel nauseous and have diarrhoea, but the sea is more amazing to me than ever before. It hits me unexpectedly quickly. I run to the toilet every ten minutes to vomit but nothing comes up. Then the sickness leaves and life is better. My mouth is constantly dry but that doesn't bother me. People tell me I look well, but I keep the secret of my new-found glow to myself. The pills keep me awake at night, but it doesn't matter because they keep me going during the day.

I wonder why it didn't work like this for Gareth. The more my life becomes normal, the worse it seems his was. The gauge of wrongness becomes tangible, not clouded in the everyday visits and the drugs and the overdoses, and the heroin requests, and the tears of one in so much turmoil.

How critical our chemical make-up is. I thought I'd lost it. Little oblong pills have given me back to myself in a chemical cover-up. One day you feel one way, the next another, courtesy of the manufactured magic. I worry what I will be like when I come off them, which I am desperate to do by now, just months later. But I'm wary in case I'm as empty as before.

And one day I do stop taking the capsule with my breakfast, needing to know if I feel the way I do because of them. The next day, when I wake up I can barely move. My head doesn't want to lift from the pillow. My body has an extreme hangover, it's cemented to the ground once I pull it out of bed. Stuck, rooted, glued, head sloshing as if it has been bashed against a wall.

My doctor tells me I should have cut back slowly. So I slice the little buggers in half with the bread knife on the chopping board. Crumbs of anti-depressant fly onto the Formica counter and I neurotically fret that their minuscule disappearance will effect the dosage and therefore me. After a few weeks I quarter them. After a few weeks of quartering, I think I must be there. I wait for my blood to turn to lead again, but it doesn't.

I haven't turned into Gareth or my mother as I thought I would. I've come back to life, and I feel like the seven-year-old girl who rode her bike on Primrose Hill as her father walked behind her, and she smiled as the breeze tousled her hair and the sun warmed her freckly face. She believed the world to be her oyster and that it could only get better with each birthday that passed.

I have only three memories before that day.

One day on the way to nursery as Mum and I passed the chip shop one of the wheels on my pushchair fell off and I thudded to the ground with such a shock that I screamed and people gathered to see why. Somehow my mother fixed the wheel back on, but it was rickety and wobbly all the way to nursery and I was convinced I would hurtle out onto the pavement at any moment.

In another, a neighbour was looking after me while my parents were out for the evening. She placed her daughter and I in a bath. Happily we dipped containers and filled them up with water so that, naturally, we could then pour the water over each other. Then I collected water straight from the tap, poured it over her and she screamed a frightful scream, sounding like a cat being strangled. As the steam rose from her skin I realized the water I'd covered her with had been burning hot. While her daughter's skin turned from white to crimson, her mother shouted at me. How could I be so stupid?

I remember, too, hearing my mother shouting and shrieking through tears in their bedroom when I was tiny. I couldn't make out what she and Dad were saying. She threw her shoes and they passed the half-closed bedroom door and fell down the stairs, clanging down, to land at my feet on the landing below. I caught glimpses of her moving around the bedroom. They were sexy, black kitten heels that she had thrown, with pointed toes and a diminutive, skimpy strap. I looked up and could see nothing. I could only hear, and what I heard was her crying like a baby and my father trying to calm her down. I looked at the shoes again, those pointy, glamorous gloves for the feet. That is the only time I heard her wailing with sadness. Other times the sadness lived in her eyes, too tired to cry, too fed up to throw shoes.

I am told of other incidents by people. How when I came home from the hospital after I was born our two cats jumped straight into my cot. One of them, Plato, was a remarkable creature. He would open our fridge with his paws and take the silver cap off each milk bottle and lick the cream away. Occasionally an irate neighbour would come round to the house to shout at my mother because Plato had got into their house, opened their fridge, and attacked their meat. Black with tabby stripes and white paws, his tail looked like it had been dipped in white paint.

Family is blood, the blood that keeps you alive, or diseased, turns out to kill you.

I know the reasons, some of them anyway, why Mum was depressed. Why she couldn't carry on. Why it was her time because she couldn't be here anymore. Why she had to go. I embrace her even though she's dead.

I wish I could wear her wedding dress, the one I threw away. Be dressed by the memory the folds of her clothes withhold. The rite of her wedding, that dress, a prop in her ceremony. How it must have absorbed her excitement, soaked up her fervour, her nervousness, her love for our father. And velvet is heavy, smoke and perfumes gather in its depths, remnants of evenings are consumed by it. But worn only once, this frock would not have known so much of my mother after all.

After fighting with her in death with fury, I remember her good. At first I struggle with this.

You left again and again, in mind and then in body.

But then it doesn't matter. Once more she is transformed for me but this time she is real. Real life woman. Absence and presence. All in one. My moments with her, I place them together and she ventures back to me. From Absent to Dead to Angel to With Me. I have her now.

Life floods into me as if I'd never known it. My body doesn't drag, it moves, and my feet are firmly rooted to the ground. They grow into it. They don't run me away, don't glide upon the past without hitting the ground. Like cats we probably have nine lives in one, and I begin another. Resilience is surprising. Any day you can wake.

The release comes unexpectedly. In knowing that two don't die when one does. In coming back to life more legitimately than before. In walking with feet that once walked next to theirs, but are fine on their own. In hearing my own voice without the echo of his screams. In the tears that dry out to make way for smiling eyes. In not having to weep to recall.

I become free from their pain and so my own is allowed to go. It had walked with me for years, left and returned, left and returned. Now it mutates into the memory of them rather than the tragedy of them.

184

For fear of losing them I had wanted to keep them alive in mind so they could stay. I went into the archaeology of recollection every day to have them here when they were gone. I wanted them to have lived longer, that they could have escaped their sadness, illnesses and depressions. I was livid they'd gone before they found the lives they might have liked. I wanted them to have years of happiness before they died. Behind my skin crawled the bitterness of their endings.

It turns into acceptance of the privilege of knowing them and the mosaic of their lives regardless of what happened. Their souls have stopped aching in me and have been digested into something beautiful which settles where before there was unrest. I give away their sadness, push it from me so that I can breathe again. The fraught nature of my thoughts dissipates and moves away from my marrow. I have found a way to stop thinking of the injustice, to wake beyond the exhaustion of a greedy grief, one which had eaten me slowly like a parasite, saving me for itself when it should have let me go. I opened windows inside me to blow away the stifling rage that seemed to have lived for an age. This doesn't happen overnight. It is not a lightening flash that brings me back, it is day by day stirrings from a coma of inertia.

I let Gareth go. More accurately, his sadness. You can carry another's depression, one that is not your own. I take his off, leave it behind, a worn-out, shed skin which deserves no one. For a while it lies waiting to be worn again, homeless as it's now disowned. So it calls on a regular basis. It aims to tear me back to how life was before, to what we're used to. But I decide to cease the fighting, the conflict which drives you into a derelict halfway house. I don't want to live with it anymore, have it be accountable for my thoughts. I want to walk without a partisan ghost behind me, one who treads on my toes when I move without pain. A constant reminder bearing the message of the past. Let it lie. I won't forget him, but I won't remember only the drama. I want the laughing and the fooling around. The laugh that cannot easily be contained. The clown's voices and faces and walks. The hilarity of feet. The blowing up of bangers. The hose pisses. The love of film and music. The fossilized dryness of his wit. Then the bad can become the understudy and the good can charm the darkness. Everything isn't heavy, the weight has gone, vanquished, left behind because that's where it belongs.

I still want to meet up with him. It is impossible not to imagine how he might be if he were alive now. Would he be different, would he be the same? Would we still be bound to expecting the next attempt? Would he be fine, helped by drugs or just a change in the chemical waltzes that took place in his brain? Would the colours of the streams of chemicals be different? Those bright scans which show our madness or our sanity. The grey on top of our spine contains over twelve million neurons, single nerve cells that transmit electrical impulses. Imagine them doing their thing. Shooting about like they own you. They do. It weighs less than three pounds. How curious that our brains can be scanned, that the chaos going on in there can be placed on a piece of paper, for all to see. The explanation is there. Someone may be going nuts, be manic beyond safety, or depressed beyond bearability, and it's all there in those scans.

Chapter Eleven

Since childhood Gareth had loved engines and things he could make move. First it was cars, then boats and then planes. He would drive the model cars up ramps he'd made in the garden, or whiz them around Hyde Park, and my mother would take him to float his remote control boats on White Stone Pond. Often they would break down in the middle of the pond after water had trespassed through a weak fibreglass join, and one of them would wade in to fish the poor boat out. He'd rev the boats in the garden to see what was wrong with the engine and stink the place out with burning oil. Then he got into model planes and they became a permanent fixture. My mother would drive him to Ivinghoe Beacon to fly his remote control gliders. He had more luck with those. They defied gravity, made their clean-cut ascent, rising to heights we couldn't reach.

Gareth once said he'd glimpsed what freedom might be like while flying one of his planes on the Beacon. He felt well as he watched the plane and the invisible striations it made in the sky. He wanted that feeling again. The appeal of being up in the air, air that somehow seemed different to the air that he breathed. Gazing with a longing that he might have read as death. Perhaps he should have been born with feathered wings. Plumage should have pierced his heated prickly skin.

Let your soul fly away. Let your pain be no more. Be released from all that kept you downtrodden here. Squashed soul like the cubes of scrap cars diminished into crushed geometry. Lose the weight of what kept you. Let your broken wings veer you to another place.

When Gareth was interviewed and assessed for a psychological report, evidence was found that he had *superior abilities which might enable him to pursue a career in some branch of aeronautics or aviation, an activity in which he is keenly interested.* In the report it is suggested that there was *an unevenness in cognitive maturation which may be secondary to his learning disability and to a history of educational failure.*

It goes on: *Gareth has a very good understanding of the physical concepts and technical aspects of aeronautics which is difficult for him to convey to the non-specialist; he seemed restricted in his expressive language so that discussion of his interest was frustrating for him. To remedy this he showed me a technical book which explained the concepts of aircraft geometry and performance sufficiently to permit a lively discussion of the relevance of such matters as dihedral angles and aspect ratios to aerobatics. It did seem to me that he was secure with these quite difficult concepts given his extensive experience of practical involvement and that he used them with great facility; I further noted his enthusiasm and pleasure in sharing an otherwise esoteric interest.*

The spare lines that gloat, those edges which rip through the air. The soaring which is like nothing felt on grass, stone or tarmac. The sky high behind the planes which murmur to those that detest the ground. The soundless motion, like an elegy on the space between him and there. He wanted to fly with them. On them, on the wind that would take him away from here. He saw them resting on airwaves, rising high above the shit he felt his life was made of. And planes leave. They go far away, run higher than feet can take you with an elegance that spelt out liberty.

Callum asked a friend of his, a very bright Reverend, if it mattered from a religious point of view if Gareth's ashes were split up. We wanted to cover his back as much as possible. He said it was unimportant and so we offered half of them to his girlfriend. She asked if she could have all of his ashes for one night, to say her own goodbye. We gave them to her, later Callum went and fetched our half.

On his way to pick me up to scatter Gareth's ashes Callum has breakfast with a friend. Whilst being extremely unlikely, he thinks about how awful it would be if the car were stolen with the ashes in it, so he brings them into the cafe and puts them on a chair, and Gareth joins the breakfast.

Then Callum and I drive to Ivinghoe Beacon to scatter them. The metal pot that houses them, courtesy of the crematorium, has a sticker on it, displaying his details. *The cremated remains of the late Gareth Alexander Gordon: 19.9.94.*

We arrive and climb the hill we'd been to with Gareth before, where others fly their planes with the same grace that Gareth did. Miniature versions of the ones leaving tracks overhead, swooping through the sky. A white boxer is there with a young couple. That's who Gareth had loved, our white boxer, and so one comes the day we throw his dust to the air. Callum has his camera, and as the ashes fall through our fingers he captures the particles falling away. We throw them to the wind but they come back to us. We throw them as high as we can only for them to fall not so far away. The boxer runs around us. It takes longer than one might think, to empty the pot of his ashes. But he is free. Free on the Beacon to go where he wants. To fly like his models once had, with a slow ease that catches rides on the tails of restless winds. We take our time, let him fall through our fingers as slowly as he wants. We throw some up to make clouds that are carried. With no great haste the grey mist of Gareth gallops in time to the wind.

Callum and Hattie